Keys to
Destiny

Life from the Inside-Out

Keys to Destiny

Life from the Inside-Out

HARVEY JOHNSON

ARPress
ILLUMINATING IDEAS
EMPOWERING VOICES

ARPress
45 Dan Road Suite 5
Canton MA 02021

Hotline: 1(888) 821-0229
Fax: 1(508) 545-7580

Ordering Information:

Quantity sales. Special discounts are available on quantity purchases by corporations,associations, and others. For details, contact the publisher at the address above.

Printed in the United States of America.

| ISBN-13: | Softcover | 979-8-89389-430-1 |
| | eBook | 979-8-89389-431-8 |

Library of Congress Control Number: 2024917276

Dedication

To Charlotte, my Wife and Co-Laborer in the ministry of Church Builders to which we have been called. She remains a source of consistent encouragement and intercession for the work we have been set apart to perform.

She is also a source of spiritual insight and partaker of these "Keys to Destiny" as God continues to pour them through our very lives as we journey together. And to my sister Maxine "Ladybug" whose Love & Support is a constant source of inspiration.

Contents

Preface..7

Acknowledgements...9

Introduction...11

1   First We Must Divide 13

2   Life from the Inside Out 22

3   "The Word Made Flesh".................................37

4   Not Alone and Not without a Struggle............51

5   Your Attachments and Relationships 57

6   Your Destiny: The Will of God 67

7   Spiritual Transition..76

8   The Kingdom of God 84

9   God's Order 86

10 The Kingdoms of this World...........................89

11 The Wisdom of God's Kingdom 91

Appendix..93

Preface

I have taught Keys to Destiny in its entirety on three separate occasions to three separate congregations. On each occasion, this writing has been refined by the presence of God for its best presentation and clarity.

This refinement includes the divine selection and order of the "Destiny Keys" and Insights that are handpicked truths, shared in order to unlock the treasures of what God has hidden inside every Life and Journey on the road to Destiny.

Also included in this refinement is a clearer approach to the definitions of <u>Purpose and Destiny</u> for the purposes of this writing.

<u>Purpose</u> is defined as the opportunities and specific task God has ordained for us to perform, in the various *Times and Seasons* of our life. Our purpose evolves as we transition through life; *It's the performance of these purposes that shape the boundaries for the realm of our destiny.*

<u>Destiny</u> is the summation of those purposes, based on a succession of experiences (journeys), that cumulates in an ultimate journey (i.e. destiny).

<u>Destiny</u> itself is not a destination that we walk into; Destiny is a realm that we have been prepared by experience to occupy and influence for the glory of God. *It's what He had in mind on the journey,* whether it is interpreted individually or corporately as our <u>Destiny</u> or <u>Ultimate Purpose</u>.

Additionally, these teachings were taped and then transcribed by Robert Bowling, a respected theologian in his own right who enhanced the refinement process by incorporating his footnotes and references, along with those inserted by myself.

You will also note that I have made mention of authors and ministers that have done works that benefit a specific subject or area covered in this writing. This includes Lance Wallnau, Peter Wagner, and John Enlow. I have made mentioned of their works or employed some of their jargon to bring clarity on the subjects of the Kingdom of God and the Kingdoms of this World.

The writing, Holy Spirit Gifts and Power by Paul Walker, contained in the Spirit Filled Life Bible: A Personal Study Bible Unveiling All God's Fullness in All God's Word (New King James Version), c1991, is also included as an appendix to support the discussion on the Gifts of the Spirit and Five Fold Ministry.

Acknowledgements

It is with Great Honor that we make mention of those spiritual gifts to the Body of Christ, whose support has proven invaluable to our cause:

Apostle Joseph and Pastor Brenda Hobbs, Triumphant Life Christian Church, we still stand upon the foundation you imparted in us.

Apostle Delphine Reed and Pastor John Dawkins, whose open understanding in the beginning helped us to demonstrate in part, what the Lord is now bringing to fullness.

Pastor Fredrick and Margaret Caldwell, Grace Community Fellowship Church, because of your personal commitment to what God showed you in us, our journey was sustained.

Senior Pastor Bruce and Pastor Monoseta Burwell, Light of the World Christian Center, who joyfully received our vision for ministry and encouraged us in our assent into the Kingdom.

Pastor Dan Rhodes founder of Destiny Navigators, whose friendship and mentoring continues to be a source of light on our path.

Pastor Jeffery K. Harvard, a faithful friend and the Greater Full Gospel COGIC; the place God chose as the launching pad for the great work of the Spirit He has prepared in us.

And most certainly our dearest friends in ministry Pastors Curtis and Katherine Savage, Broken Vessels Ministries.

Introduction

This writing was delivered to me by the Spirit of God, many years, before I was fully aware of its becoming in my own life. After years of prayer and experience, life itself has coauthored its conception and completion. So it is with great joy that I am fully released to put pen to paper, with the "Eyes of My Understanding Opened" and now able to share this with you.

Though it's been years since it was first introduced into my heart, I feel that it is now being released as a "Word in Season" for your reading after God has prepared both the writing and the writer in one vessel for your edification.

"**Keys to Destiny**" is not only a Word of Wisdom and Knowledge to the Body of Christ, but also a road map for every soul that is thirsting for purpose, destiny, and a framework that will help establish the desires of their heart.

Although many years have been poured into in their formation, the keys and insights found in this writing are presented in concise and relevant portions for believers and seekers at every level. To further ease their absorption I have summarized some of the "Keys and Insights" at the end of every section and made room for each reader to document their own "Personal Keys, Insights, and Notes" as the Spirit speaks to them.

My prayer is that you would let these living words extracted from a heart committed to delivering life changing truths to all that would hear them; in order to motivate, elevate, and propel you forward into your destiny, no matter what age or season you are experiencing at the moment you hear them.

"**Keys to Destiny**" is not all the truth you will ever need, but some jewels to add to the treasures that your life is gathering "Along the Way."

Chapter 1

First We Must Divide

"And God saw the light, that [it was] good: and God
divided the light from the darkness." (Gen. 1:4 KJV).

In Genesis chapter one verse, 1 we find these familiar words; many
people know them, and every disciple needs to be reminded of them.

> Gen. 1:1 says, "In the beginning, God created the heavens and
> the earth.[1]

When God created the earth, it was good, it was perfect, it was a
paradise and God had a plan and a purpose for it. The thing that we
must discern is what happened between verse 1 and verse 2 because

> Gen. 1:2 says, "And the earth was without form, and void; and
> darkness [was] upon the face of the deep."

We have to pause after verse one to gain understanding, because
verse 2 is not how God created the heavens and the earth.

Do you think God created a world that was without form? Does
that sound like His work? Is this the reason we seek a relationship

---

[1] The Dateless Past: Marking the boundary between time and eternity, aprox.6,
000 years before the creation of man in Genesis chapter one (*Dake's Annotated
Reference Bible*).

with Him, for a life without form and void, with darkness upon its depth? God didn't do that, something had to have happen!

Between verse 1 and verse 2, Satan described as (Lucifer) fell from heaven. And he fell to an earth that God had made good, and he caused it to become formless, void, and covered in darkness.

In the book of Isaiah 14:12–16 we read,

Isaiah 14:12 KJV, "How art thou fallen from heaven, O Lucifer, son of the morning! [how] art thou cut down to the ground, which didst weaken the nations!"

Isaiah 14:13 KJV, "For thou hast said in thine heart, I will ascend into heaven, I will exalt my throne above the stars of God: I will sit also upon the mount of the congregation, in the sides of the north."

Isaiah 14:14 KJV, "I will ascend above the heights of the clouds; I will be like the most High."

Isaiah 14:15 KJV, "Yet thou shalt be brought down to hell, to the sides of the pit."

Isaiah 14:16 KJV, "They that see thee shall narrowly look upon thee, [and] consider thee, [saying, Is] this the man that made the earth to tremble, that did shake kingdoms."

And in Luke 10:18 it says,

Luke 10:18 KJV, "And he said unto them, I beheld Satan as lightning fall from heaven."

I beheld Satan as lightning fall from heaven. This is Jesus speaking in the New Testament that he watched Satan fall; he watched as God dispelled him from heaven.

The reason Satan fell from the presence of God is pride, as revealed in his **five I will's** captured in Isaiah 14:12–16. The devil wants to be like God. He wants to rule over the things God has created, especially mankind.

The devil wants to rule over what God has created because he does not have the power create anything for himself.

Satan can't create anything. He can only attempt to rearrange or reform what has already been created, making true what the Bible says that, "No weapon formed against us shall prosper" and if we pay close attention to our spiritual conflicts, we will notice in the spiritual challenges, that most often oppose us, are usually the same problem in a different form.

In Genesis 1:2 and the verses that follow we see God inserting Himself, because what God intended to be good and orderly, the devil has fallen upon and made it dark and chaotic.

How does God fix the problem? Gen 1:2 says, "And the Spirit of God moved upon the face of the waters."

The Spirit brings our chaotic situations into the Presence and the Word of God. God's Presence is the place and the source of all original intent, design, and purposes of His Will. In the book of Genesis, God shows us how to expose and remove the *Formlessness* (Dysfunction), *the Void* (Invalidation), and the *Darkness* (Hopelessness) from our life, by teaching us the Methodology of the Spirit.

At first observation, you would think that God who has the power would have begun by removing the devil from the place of His Will, but in the beginning from the book of Genesis, God reveals to us His Thoughts and His Ways. God has a spiritual problem, and He solves it spiritually.

The first act of God in the Bible is an act of **Spiritual Warfare.** The objective of this warfare was the "Restoration of the original intent, plans, and purposes of God's will" which should be the objective of all our "Spiritual Battles."

The **Purpose** of this Restoration was the coming of **Adam** and God's plan for man.

In Genesis 1:3 when God responds to the formlessness, the void, and the darkness, He starts with the proclamation, "Let there be light[2]: and there was light."

---

[2] **Let there be light**, is the command that releases the power of God upon the earth, to remove the darkness, restore the earth back to God's Original intent and bring it into alignment with His already existing will.

DESTINY KEY

In the list of the Spiritual gifts that are listed in 1ˢᵗ Corinthians chapter 12, the first gift is **WORD OF WISDOM**[3]. A **Word of Wisdom** is a <u>Supernatural Disclosure</u> expressed by the Spirit. **A Word of Wisdom** is the divine means for accomplishing God's will in a given situation. When you have a **Word of Wisdom**, you have the "**Mind of God**" concerning the specific need or event disclosed: It is God's wisdom working interactively with knowledge and discernment; Divine Knowledge rightly applied.

There is an existing **Word of Wisdom** that discloses; <u>the Mind of God concerning our finances, the Mind of God concerning our marriage,</u> and <u>the mind of God concerning the circumstances</u> that we are facing. The first gift of the spirit is the **Word of Wisdom**, and in any situation or circumstance, what we need to know is **what does God thinks about what we are experiencing?** When we have a **Word of Wisdom** we have the arsenal of God's will against the thing that opposes "His Purpose" for our life.

In Genesis 1:3 God is showing us the power of "Revealed Truth." Genesis 1:3 says, "And God said, let there be light: and there was light."

The problem was darkness in the place that God intended light. God could have fixed everything at once with the hand of his power, but he dealt with the problem with the word that it needed. He didn't call for angels or cause the heavens to open up. He didn't do any of that. He spoke the original intent of God with the "Word of Wisdom:" "Let there be light."

When God says "Let" there be Light," He's releasing Divine Illumination. <u>This is not sunlight that will occur in Genesis 1:14 on</u>

---

[3] **See Appendix Holy Spirit Gifts and Power by Paul Walker,** Spirit filled life study Bible. 1997, c1991 (electronic ed.) Re 22:18). Nashville: Thomas Nelson;

day four, but this is Divine Light from the presence of God released on day one.

Once we establish the Light of God from His Presence, everything that's not light, (that's not like Him), becomes exposed so we can see the real cause of our battle. **Let's retrace God's steps!**

First, God applies the "Spirit" to the problem. Then out of the Spirit He speaks, "God said." In Genesis 1:1–23, God repeats the phrase "God said" ten times, and ten times it produced the same results, "And it was so."

The observation is that "The Spirit Moved, God Spoke, and Things Changed." But God just didn't speak "A Word;" God spoke "The Word" for the situation at hand.

When He called for light, He spoke the mind and will of His original intent. He spoke his prophetic insight and purpose back into the place He had created. In another scripture 1 Timothy Chapter 1:18, Paul reminds Timothy to fight a good warfare with the power of the prophecy that was spoken over his ministry. First Tim. 1:18 KJV, "This charge I commit unto thee, son Timothy, according to the prophecies which went before on thee, that thou by them mightiest war a good warfare."

In other words, Paul was saying to Timothy, "When you run into opposition about your ministry or your calling, "Pray your Prophecy," pray the intent, and "Will of God."

Find the **Word of Wisdom** God has for your marriage, the word God revealed to you about your ministry, the word God spoke over your life and speak that word to the thing that is coming against the mind, will, and intent of God. This is called speaking Truth to Power. Aside from "truth" everything else has an expiration date and will eventually cease to exist, but truth is eternal in its origin; only the truth can and will make us free.

> After this, in Genesis 1:4, it says, "And God saw the light, that [it was] good: and God divided the light from the darkness."

God Divided, so should we. "**We must divide**" our battlefields with a word of wisdom for each challenge in our life, or we will experience overlap in seeking answers and applying solutions to our conflicts. We will find ourselves fussing with our wife or husband about a situation, that is really a problem we are having with our children or inflicting controversy upon our family because of a chal-lenge we're facing on our job. We must divide our battle grounds to maintain and deploy effectual Spiritual Strategies and Focus, so that the enemy will not overwhelm us by provoking us to swallow the whole elephant or bite off the wrong piece.

Nor can we allow ourselves to chase after the symptoms. For example: If our warfare is against a lying spirit in one of our loved ones, it goes beyond the lies that are being told; it could have its ori-gin in the person's childhood. First, it was the cookies missing from the cookie jar, but as they grew older it was about the homework they didn't complete, or the test scores they hid. After they got married it was about where they were last night.

Same problem just in a different form, the problem has reformed itself as they grew older. It's unfortunate that the person keeps lying, but in the movement of the Spirit and Presence of God we can find out why he/she is a liar. What reality is it that they can't face that makes them lie? In the Spirit we can find out what the true cause of their lying is.

But not just dividing outwardly, we must also search inwardly, to see how our challenges are impacting us.

Gen 1:2 says, "And the earth was without form, and void; and darkness [was] upon the face of the deep."

The state of **Formlessness** is to be without a definitive design, being **Void** means to be invalidated or without value, and to be **Covered in Darkness** is the absence of light, not seeing any oppor-tunity or options for change.

These physical states exist when things or people take on the shape of the circumstances they are in, **like water takes on the shape of whatever it's poured it into**;

- pour it into a pitcher and *it looks like the pitcher*;
- Pour it into a jelly jar and *it looks like the jelly jar.*
- If you put it in a bottle cap *it looks very small,* if you pour it into a bucket *it looks large.*

> But the truth of the matter is, no matter what shape it's poured into, it's still **"Water", with all of the life giving qualities it was created with; in spite of the circumstances it has been poured into**. No matter what circumstances we are in, at our core; we are still the "Will of God" in the earth realm.

If opposing spirits can get us to attempt to solve everything at once, too many things at one time or the symptom instead of the true cause of the problem, we will feel like we're without form; we're going to feel void, and it's going to seem like we are lost in a state of darkness. The three basic weapons of satanic influence are **Deception, Distraction, and Darkness**.

If the enemy can cause us to feel formless, void, and covered in darkness by deception, distraction, and darkness, he will attempt to dictate who we are, by impressing upon our thought-life things like "You're not the father you're supposed to be," "You have no authority in your house," "You're not a woman of God," "You didn't hear from God," "Your prayers don't work," but when it comes to spiritual conflicts, no matter what shape they take—Formlessness, Void or Darkness—God will reveal the solution for the problem.

God is "All Powerful" He did not need six days to reassemble the earth and create man, but in the beginning (Genesis), His works are performed in this six-day format in order to reveal the Keys to our Destiny and His Principles to what must be done in our spiritual battles. God reassembles the earth and creates man in this slowed down process, so that we can catch the revelation of His Will by the His Spirit.

By the Spirit of God we must come into His Presence, receive, and decree the revealed Word of God for the warfare that we are encountering.

By the Light of God (Spiritual Understanding) we must divide our battle fields in order to gain Divine Insight and Focus, in order to effectually deploy God's Strategies.

We really can't talk about advancement in the Kingdom of God without that type of spiritual relationship with "God and His Word." We must be able to communicate with God, but we can't communicate with God effectively, without operating in His Spirit because God is a Spirit.

I'm not saying that God doesn't understand our words when we pray with own understanding or when we're overwhelmed. God understands our words, our thoughts, and our feelings before we speak or feel them, but when we talk about the Spiritual Matters of Divine Destiny and Purpose in our life, we must enter into that Spiritual Realm.

We must not only be "Lead by the Spirit," but we must "Walk (Advance) in the Spirit" by which we are being led.

Beloved of God, please understand that just because you experience spiritual opposition doesn't mean you're a bad person. It just means that you're being opposed.

Now that we have identified the "Operation of the Spirit" as God's weapon of choice, against the true nature of our enemy "We Must Divide." I would like to point out four dimensions of this warfare.

The first dimension of our warfare is our "Inner Man," the "Life we live from within;" the second dimension is our "Outer Man" or the Image of God on our life. The third dimension we must observe is "Our Attachments" and "Key Relationships," and the fourth dimension is "Our Destiny" or God's ultimate purpose for our life.

Destiny Keys and Insights

The first act of God in the Bible is an "Act of Spiritual Warfare." The "Objective" of this warfare was the "Restoration of the Will, Plans, and Intent of God."

Satan can't create anything. He can only attempt to rearrange or reform what has already been created. That's why the Bible says, "No weapon formed against us shall prosper."

God is All Powerful and did not need six days to reassemble the earth and create man, but in the beginning, in the book of Genesis, His works are performed is this six-day format in order to reveal the Keys to our Destiny and His Spiritual Principles.

My Keys

_____

_____

My Insights and Notes

_____
_____
_____
_____
_____
_____
_____
_____
_____
_____
_____
_____

Chapter 2

Our Inner Man:
"Life from the Inside Out"

Lord, as we turn our face, our hearts, and our minds toward you, we pray that all things that we are currently experiencing circumstantially, physically, mentally or spiritually in our lives be delivered unto a greater understanding and knowledge of who you are in us. We know that you have only the highest good and the highest purpose for us. We say thank you for being our Lord and our God. Now, Lord, open our hearts, our minds, and our ears so that we might receive the Word, the Spirit, and the Revelation of "Your Will" regarding The Keys to Our Destiny, that we might be edified and made ready for your service, in Jesus name, Amen…

Now we're going to begin our journey into the "The Keys to Our Destiny" with the warfare over our "inner man." Once again we look at 1 Corinthians the twelfth chapter and the eighth through the eleventh verse, where Paul describes the following:

Gifts of the Spirit

First Corinthians 12:8 KJV, "For to one is given by the Spirit the word of wisdom; to another the word of knowledge by the same Spirit."

First Corinthians 12:9 KJV, "To another faith by the same Spirit; to another the gifts of healing by the same Spirit"

First Corinthians 12:10 KJV, "To another the working of miracles; to another prophecy; to another discerning of spirits; to another [divers] kinds of tongues; to another the interpretation of tongues."

First Corinthians 12:11 KJV, "But all these worketh that one and the selfsame Spirit, dividing (Measured) to every man severally as he will."

First Corinthians 12 concludes with verse 31. Where in Paul's comment he desires us to consider a more excellent way. First Corinthians 12:31 KJV, "But covet earnestly the best gifts: and yet shew I unto you a more excellent way."

Paul carries this thought into chapter 13, where he takes us into a deeper understanding of "Love" which is also the first dimension of the Fruit of the Spirit listed in Galatians chapter 5, verses 22 and 23;

Fruit of the Spirit

Galatians 5:22–23 KJV, "But the fruit of the Spirit is love, joy, peace, longsuffering, gentleness, goodness." Galatians 5:23 KJV, "Meekness, faith and temperance: against such there is no law."

Galatians 5, verses 24–26 goes on to say;

Galatians 5:24 KJV, "And they that are Christ's have crucified the flesh with the affections and lusts."

Galatians 5:25 KJV, "If we live in the Spirit, let us also walk in the Spirit."

In other words if we "Live in the Gifts" we should "Walk in the Fruit" (Galatians 5:25 paraphrased).

- In Galatians 5:22–23 Paul listed the nine dimensions of a single Fruit: love, joy, peace, long suffering, gentleness, goodness, meekness, faith, temperance, and then states that against such there is no law (no limits), and they that are Christ have crucified the flesh with the affection of the lust. (*The exchange rate of the Spirit is flesh, in order to advance in the spirit, something in the flesh must decease*).

- Likewise In 1 Corinthians 12:8–11 Paul presents nine gifts of a single Spirit.

Here the Holy Spirit and Word of God bless us with the knowledge that, in order to magnify the nine Gifts of the Spirit that are mentioned in 1 Corinthians chapter 12:8–11, the more excellent way is to walk in the Fruit of the Spirit, listed in Gal 5:22–23, by crucifying the flesh.

As we have noted there are nine Gifts of the Spirit listed in 1 Corinthians 12. For review let's read them. First is the Word of Wisdom, word of knowledge, the gift of faith, gifts of healing, the working of miracles, prophecy, discerning spirits, different kinds of tongues, and the interpretation of tongues.

Destiny Key

The Gifts of the Spirit are quickened and restored to us upon our being "saved and sealed by the Holy Spirit" at our redemption. Our gifts are determined in God's predestined will, the place of their origin, we have done nothing to earn them; they are Gifts.

In 2 Corinthians 1:22, it says, "Who hath also sealed us, and given the earnest[4] of the Spirit in our hearts."

God seals us in our gift(s) because God already knows who we are in Him, before we are able to fully understand who He is in us. These gifts may also be identified and can be activated in the operations of the five-fold ministry gifts outlined by Christ in Ephesians (4:10–15).

The Fruit of the Spirit is the character and nature of God that is developed in us overtime and pruned for growth at every new level. By its very nature, fruit takes time and seasons for its perfecting. The Fruit and Gifts of the Spirit established in us are not just for us, but for the people and places we serve on behalf of God.

---

[4] Earnest: ur'-nest (arrhabon): There is more than just the idea of security from a single act in this word; it implies the continuity and identity of a continued Blessing by an observing Blesser.

INSIGHT

There does not have to be a special occasion or church service for these gifts to be made manifest, but **when the Church comes together these gifts should be present and operating in and through us,** and should be welcomed in the corporate settings of the church. When the Body of Christ is functioning in its true spiritual intent, these gifts are in operation, but what we have just discovered is that a hindrance in the operation of the "**Gifts of the Spirit**" may be a malfunction in **"Fruits of the Spirit" Love** being the key motive. Paul lets us know that the "**More Excellent Way**" 1Cr 12:31 is walking in a balance between **the Fruit** (The Character and Nature of God) and **the Gifts** from (The Spirit of God).

With that foundation being laid, we can go forward and make our way into a deeper understanding of the "Battle" over our Inner Man. So far we have considered 1 Corinthians chapter 12, with Galatians chapter 5, so now let's go to Romans 8:5–11.

Romans 8:5 KJV, "For they that are after the flesh do mind the things of the flesh; but they that are after the Spirit the things of the Spirit."

Romans 8:6 KJV, "For to be carnally minded [is] death; but to be spiritually minded [is] life and peace."

(This is a comparison between the carnal mind, (being self-conscious or world conscious) versus being spiritually minded or (God conscious.)

Romans 8:7 KJV, "Because the carnal mind [is] enmity against God: for it is not subject to the law of God, neither indeed can be."

Romans 8:8 KJV, "So then they that are in the flesh cannot please God."

Romans 8:9 KJV, "But ye are not in the flesh, but in the Spirit, if so be that the Spirit of God dwell in you."

Romans 8:10 KJV, "And if Christ [be] in you, the body [is] dead because of sin; but the Spirit [is] life because of righteousness."

Rom 8:11 KJV, "But if the Spirit of him that raised up Jesus from the dead dwell in you, he that raised up Christ from the dead shall also quicken your mortal bodies by his Spirit that dwelleth in you."

When we look at the book of Romans chapter 8, we must consider the work of the Holy Spirit in our Inner Man. *Remember that the Spirit is God's weapon of choice against the works of the enemy (Gen 1:2).*

Insight

The Holy Spirit is mentioned one time in the first seven chapters of the book of Romans, but is mentioned nineteen times in chapter 8. Paul makes a pivotal turn concerning spiritual matters in the life of the believer as he sets the "Mind of the Spirit" and the "Mind of the flesh" in contrast with one another, so that we can make an accurate analogy, of our Spiritual walk and the life we now live with God.

We are spiritual beings and must understand as God's vessels, that we are in a battle, whether we want to be or not, whether we join the choir, the usher board or the deacon board; the Pentecostal, Methodist or Baptist church, once we put on the spiritual identity of our salvation we become an enemy of the flesh. Paul takes chapter 8 to swing our thought process, our mind sets and spiritual focus inwardly to the spiritual gravity in which we are govern by God. God governs our hearts and orders our steps by the work of the Holy Spirit in us.

Romans 8:7 says the carnal mind is enmity against God therefore it is not subject (Will not Submit) to the law of God, which is the "Word of God" and neither can it be. That word enmity is here in Romans 8:7 and has its origin in the book of Genesis, and we're going to go there, but first let's look at Galatians 5:17:

Gal 5:17 KJV, "For the flesh lusteth against the Spirit, and the Spirit against the flesh: and these are contrary the one to the other: so that ye cannot do the things that ye would."

So you can't do what you want to do for God, if you are a servant of your flesh. This is in the same context of Romans 8:7 that the flesh (un-submitted) and the Spirit stand at opposition in our inner man.

Destiny Key

We are delivered from the opposing mindset, the Carnal mind, when our mind is renewed by the Spirit according to (Rom 12:2) and what we just read in Romans 8 and Galatians 5.

Some of the ways to discern the Carnal mind's activity is that, the carnal mind is self-seeking, self-promoting, and pursues instant gratification; it just wants what it sees; says what's on its mind; or does what it's feeling in the moment, without considering the impact on others or God's bigger picture for their life.

Instant gratification even though it feels right for the moment, the consequences will have to be paid further down the road. The Carnal Mind settles for the satisfaction of the moment and doesn't want to wait for its season.

On the other hand, one of the key indications of the "Spiritual mind or Mind of the Spirit" is that it has a patient and seasonal nature like the character of God and able to endure the process (of seed, time, and harvest) Gen 8:22. That's why one dimension of the Fruit of the Spirit is *long suffering*.

Let's summarize what we've just read. The mind of the flesh is opposed to the mind of the spirit.

In this life and in our present state in the earth realm, these two things will never be in a place of agreement. We will never encounter any season or situation in our life, where the flesh and the Spirit are on the same page. The proper place for our flesh is to be submitted to the "Mind of the Spirit" that dwells within us.

When Paul points us to *a more excellent way* in 1 Corinthians 12:31 and introduces us to Galatians chapter 5 he teaches us about the balance that is needed between the Fruit and the Gifts of the Spirit. Paul also makes us aware of the Enmity of the Carnal Mind against God.

We know that Paul is the author of all three books Corinthians, Galatians, and Romans, so we need to see the source from where Paul is getting his information and why this is so crucial to us in our inner spiritual battles.

So now we are going to the book of Genesis to find the origin of this enmity and how the warfare got started. In Genesis 3:14–15 we find the source of the word enmity that is the foundation of where Paul led us in Romans 8:7.

Genesis 3:14 KJV, "And the LORD God said unto the serpent, because thou hast done this, thou [art] cursed above all cattle, and above every beast of the field; upon thy belly shalt thou go, and dust shalt thou eat all the days of thy life."

Gen 3:15 KJV, "And I will put Enmity between thee and the woman, and between thy seed and her seed; it shall bruise thy head, and thou shalt bruise his heel."

That word **enmity** means intense hatred, to be hostile toward, to war against, and oppose. Like the families of the Hatfield's and the McCoy's because they were at war with each other, you couldn't put them in the same space because it was just a matter of time before they were going to go to battle.

It's the same way between the flesh and the Spirit you can't put them in the same space. They're hostile toward each other. The book of Romans says that, if you walk in the spirit you won't fulfill the lust of flesh, but it also says that the flesh is enmity against the spirit.

Insight

The Bible says in Gen 3:1 KJV, "Now the serpent was more **subtil**[5] than any beast of the field which the LORD God had made. And he said unto the woman, Yea, hath God said, ye shall not eat of every tree of the garden?" So it is for us today, Satan makes sin logical to the carnal mind/flesh. Remembering what we previously exposed about the three major objectives of the enemy, Deception, Distraction and Darkness. He is probably going to try to deceive you, distract you from the truth you already know, or cast your life into darkness, so you can see no light, He does this to carry us into the most hopeless state possible from what we are experiencing, so that we can't see the help God has placed within us and to cause us to seek some source other than God.

The verses we read in Genesis 3:14–15 is after the fall of Adam. Eve has delivered unto Adam the forbidden fruit, Adam has consumed it, and now God is handing out the verdicts.

So the serpent deceives Eve, and God says to the serpent in Genesis 3:14, "Because thou hast done this, thou [art] cursed above all cattle, and above every beast of the field; upon thy belly shalt thou go, and dust shalt thou eat all the days of thy life."

Now look at verse 15, this is the first time we see this word enmity. Genesis 3:15, "And I will put enmity between thee and the woman, and between thy seed and her seed." Do you see that?

Let's look at the Seed. When talking about the "seed of the woman," it's a person. That seed was and is Jesus and any manifestation of who He is, including His Spirit. The opposing seed is the seed of the serpent. The seed of the Serpent is the manifestation of his plots, schemes or snares, carried out by anybody he can get to do

---

[5] Subtil (spelled subtle), this means that the serpent was Crafty, Cunning, and Artful at masking the consequences of sin.

his work, <u>the children of darkness</u>, or any place in our life where he can get us to submit to his will.

If the devil needs a lie to be told, he has to find some wiling or weak soul to be a liar for him. That's the seed of the enemy. He won't do it himself; in fact, he can't do it himself, that's the Law (Covenant) of Adam[6]. Only Adam; rightly or wrongly has been given dominion in the earth Gen 1: 26-28.

Now you may ask, how did we get mixed up in this? Many people think it's because of Adam's fall, and to some degree that is true. But the real challenge is that when we got saved, we got sealed with the same spirit that raised Jesus from the dead [7](The Seed of the Woman), and have become the children of Light.

> Romans 8:11 says, "But if the Spirit of him that raised up Jesus from the dead dwell in you, he that raised up Christ from the dead shall also quicken your mortal bodies by his Spirit that dwelleth in you.

This manifestation of the Spirit in us, when we got saved, created a separation from our flesh, while at the same time giving us access to the "Presence and Manifestation of God" in our life.

Here we receive better understanding of the occurrence of Rented Veil at the Crucifixion of Jesus where we received access to God and our ultimate victory that now exists in the risen Christ, the Anointed One and His Anointing in us.

---

[6] Since Adam (translated—mankind) was given dominion by God in Gen1:26, 28; He alone has authority to speak or rule over the earth realm. In order for another spirit being to speak or operate with the authority that mankind was given, he must find an Adam to do so for him.

[7] After the Advent of the birth, death, burial and resurrection of Jesus Christ; He was given all authority in heaven and in Earth (Mat 28:18), and now those who speak in His name (Representatives Sealed in His Spirit) have God's authority in the earth.

> In Matthew 27:51 KJV, we read that after Jesus cried, "It Is Finished;" "And, behold, the veil of the temple was rent in twain from the top to the bottom; and the earth did quake, and the rocks rent."

This rented veil is in the temple designed by God, built by Moses, and stood between the people and access to the "Most Holy Place" and direct relationship with God, according to Hebrews 9:3.

> Hebrews 9:3 KJV, "And after the second veil, the tabernacle which is called the Holiest of all."

The rented veil is an outward symbol of the inward work of the Holy Spirit inside every believer who has become the temple of God. The rented veil now dwells inside of us!

Ephesians 2:13–16 explains the end of the enmity that has been sealed in us according to what we read in Rom 8:11.

> Ephesians. 2:13 KJV, "But now in Christ Jesus ye who sometimes were far off are made nigh by the blood of Christ."
>
> Ephesians 2:14 KJV, "For he is our peace, who hath made both one, and hath broken down the middle wall of partition [between us]."

Ephesians 2:15 KJV, "Having abolished in his flesh the **enmity**, [even] the law of commandments [contained] in ordinances; for to make in himself of twain one new man, [so] making peace."

Ephesians 2:16 KJV, "And that he might reconcile both unto God in one body by the cross, having slain the enmity thereby."

And Hebrews 10:20 lets us know that "by a new and living way, which he hath consecrated for us, through the veil, that is to say, his flesh ..."

The same spirit that raised Jesus up from the dead now resides in you. These two entities, the Spirit of Light and the spirit of darkness are in opposition to one another, as a matter of fact light and darkness can't occupy the same space. Ultimately "Light" will rule over darkness in every situation. The darkness does not rule because it has been defeated by the light and darkness can only exist where there is no light.

So we have these factions at war, one is what we got sealed with when we got saved, the (Holy Spirit).

Ephesians 1:13 KJV, "In whom ye also [trusted], after that ye heard the word of truth, the gospel of your salvation: in whom also after that ye believed, ye were sealed with that Holy Spirit of promise."

The other when we were born of the flesh:

John 3:6 KJV, "That which is born of the flesh is flesh; and that which is born of the Spirit is spirit."

As we mature in the Spirit, we will conquer the struggle inside of us by bringing it under subjection to the Spirit. The inner access to God's presence will create God's image on the outward expression of our life and when the enemy sees or hears the image of God in our life he deploys *deception*, *distraction*, and *darkness* to hinder, obstruct or deny us the victory that has already been won. When Christ, the revealed Image of God shows up on the outside and becomes apparent on your life, you become a candidate for the schemes of the enemy, but you are empowered by the Spirit of God for the victory in every instance and at every level.

Destiny Keys and Insights

"The Gifts of the Spirit" are quickened and restored to us upon our being Sealed by the Holy Spirit at our redemption.

The *Fruit of the Spirit* is the character of God that is acquired and developed *seasonally* overtime and is pruned for regrowth at every new level.

We are delivered from the opposing mindset, the Carnal mind, when our mind is renewed by the Spirit according to (Rom 12:2).

Satan is *subtle* and seeks to make sin seem logical and without consequence to the carnal mind/flesh. The three major objectives of the enemy are deception, distraction, and darkness.

My Keys

_____

_____

My Insights and Notes

_____
_____
_____
_____
_____
_____
_____
_____
_____

Chapter 3

"The Word Made Flesh"

So far we have covered the reasons why "We Must Divide" and our "Inner Man" and the life we live from within. Now we will consider our outer man or the "Image of God" on our life, followed by Our Attachments and Relationships. Just remember that the Inner Man is the deepest part of you; it's the place where God abides in us. It is the workshop of the Lord, the place where He invests "His Treasures" in us. 2 Corinthians 4:7 KJV, tells us ("we have this treasure in earthen vessels that the Excellency of the power may be of God, and not of us.")

To be clear on this point, we must understand that without the progression of our Inner Man, the outer aspects of our Destiny become very difficult to approach, because all of the attributes of God—His Understanding, Wisdom, and Revelation—along with the Gifts and Fruit of the Spirit are all accomplished in our "Inner Man."

According to Psalms 51:6, the desire of God for us, is that we possess these truths in the hidden part of our Inner Man.

Psalms 51:6 KJV, : Behold, thou desirest truth in the inward parts: and in the hidden [part] thou shalt make me to know wisdom."

As we look at the "The Image of God" on our life, we read in Gen 1:26: "God said, Let us make man in our image, after

our likeness: and let them have dominion." Three things must
be considered here:

1. Where God says, "Let us make man in our image." God is
   a Triune yet unified entity (Father, Son, and Holy Spirit).
   Man made in God's image refers to man being created as a
   Tripartite[8] or a three part being; Spirit, Soul, and Body. As
   man's creator, God is concerned with all three[9] dimensions
   of man's image[9].
2. If you think about the phrase "After our likeness," in one
   sense means a reflection, as an image in a mirror. In another
   sense it means to follow after as in a type and shadow of
   God. When God looked at man He wanted to see Himself,
   but not just a reflection of who God is; God also wanted to
   see man as a shadow following after the thoughts and ways
   of God's movements.
3. "Let them have dominion." Let "them" refers to Adam and
   Eve being one, as the "Body of Christ" is one, revealing the
   divine nature of their union; remember Eve was a mystery
   hidden in the body of Adam as the Church is a mystery hidden in "Body of Christ." Let them have "Dominion" based
   on their divine Creation, Order, and Alignment, with each
   other and the will of God in heaven, not domination, but
   dominion by strategic positioning as Eve was strategically
   hidden in Adam.

---

[8] Tripartite Man: Man is a tri-partite being—spirit, soul, and body. It is with his
Spirit that a man worships, and may contact God. The Soul includes the conscious
and subconscious minds, the realm of emotions and the will. The Soul also gives a
man personality, self-awareness, rationality and natural feeling. The Body is a com-
plex physical creation by which a person relates to this world and to other people in
the world. God is interested in all three portions of our being—spirit, soul, and body.
[9] 1 Th. 5:23 KJV, "And the very God of peace sanctify you wholly; and [I pray
God] your whole spirit and soul and body be preserved blameless unto the coming
of our Lord Jesus Christ."

In the natural we understand that many of us have the image of our own family. They say you look like your grandfather or you look like your aunt or some other family member. Once we were looking at pictures of my youngest son when he was three or four years old and it's amazing, his son looks just like him when he was at that same age. They were the spitting image of each other. Even though they were born in different eras, a span of time that covered over forty years, they still looked alike. That's how powerful our bloodline image can be, but just think how much more powerful the image of God is on our lives. <u>The image of God is a projection from our</u> Inner Man onto our Outer Man, where people see what's on the inside of us, as it is revealed on the outside of us. **Our life and our destiny in God, is lived from the inside-out.**

When God is at the center of who you are, at the center of your going out and your coming in, at the center of your motives and your desires, people will not just see a reflection of God in your life, they will see a projection of God on the canvas of your flesh.

They see "**The Word Made Flesh.**" In the New Testament, in the Gospel of John in the first chapter we read these words, John 1:1–5.

John 1:1, "In the beginning was the Word, and the Word was with God, and the Word was God."

John 1:2, "The same was in the beginning with God.

John 1:3, "All things were made by him; and without him was not anything made that was made."

John 1:4, "In him was life; and the life was the light of men."

John 1:5, "And the light shineth in darkness; and the darkness comprehended it not."

The significance of John's writings is that he writes after all others have written; He is the last writer in our Bible. The Gospel of John is a type of New Testament Genesis. It recaptures the things that God performed, but it also reintroduces us to the truth that Jesus was the Word, that was with God in the beginning. When we began on our journey into destiny, we started with the book of Genesis and saw God repair the earth realm that had been desecrated because of Satan's fall from the heaven to the Earth. God had created the earth good, but when Satan fell his demonic presence perverted God's intentions for the Earth.

How did God fix the Earth? He spoke, and so when they say in John 1:1, "In the beginning was the Word, and the Word was with God, and the Word was God." When God spoke, what He spoke was Jesus, the "Word of God," the incarnate and expressed "mind and will of God."

Destiney Key

When we talk about "The Word Made Flesh" it speaks to two points, the first being Jesus Humanity, a specific point in time when he walked the earth, a window of opportunity for us to witness what God intended for man, The gospel of John goes on to say; John 1:14 "And we beheld his glory, the glory as of the only begotten of the Father, full of grace and truth.

The Word Made Flesh also points to our relationship with Christ's Divinity: Hebrews 2:11, "For both he that sanctifieth and they who are sanctified [are] all of one: for which cause he is not ashamed to call them brethren."

Hebrews 2:12, saying, "I will declare thy name unto my brethren, in the midst of the church will I sing praise unto thee."

Hebrews 2:13, "And again, I will put my trust in him. And again, Behold I and the children which God hath given me."

The Word made flesh is the multidimensional expression of "revealed truth." It is God fulfilling His glory in the Sons of God.

In the book of Revelations that was also written by John we find these words:

> Revelations 19:11 KJV, "And I saw heaven opened, and behold a white horse; and he that sat upon him [was] called Faithful and True, and in righteousness he doth judge and make war."
>
> Revelations 19:12 KJV, "His eyes [were] as a flame of fire, and on his head [were] many crowns; and he had a name written, that no man knew, but he himself."
>
> Revelations 19:13 KJV, "And he [was] clothed with vesture dipped in blood: and his name is called The Word of God."

The gospel of John goes on to say in John 1:2, "The same was in the beginning with God, He was the mind of God, He was God's thoughts being caught in the framework of His Creative Expression. Before the world ever was, it was a thought in the mind of God. From the text in John 1:1 to Revelations 19:11–13 John takes us in the conciseness of his words from creation to a place of revelation beyond the cross, letting us know that as God spoke, Jesus the Word of God worked the works.

John 1:3, "All things were made by him; and without him was not anything made that was made. There is nothing that was made that He did not make."

The creative Word of God has the Wisdom of God in it; that's why Proverbs 8:1, 3, and 22 says;

> Proverbs 8:1, "Doth not wisdom cry? And understanding put forth her voice?"
>
> Proverbs 8:3, "She crieth at the gates, at the entry of the city, at the coming in at the doors."
>
> Proverbs 8:22, "The LORD possessed me in the beginning of his way, before his works of old."

When God speaks, and we receive the Truth in our inner man, that truth comes with the Wisdom of God in it.

The Gospel of John goes on to say of Jesus and His earthly ministry;

> John 1:4, "In him was life; and the life was the light of men."
>
> John 1:5, "And the light shineth in darkness; and the darkness comprehended it not."

Darkness is the absence of light. Darkness, in and of itself, really has no power. If we cut off the power source, for a building … there will not be any light on the inside. The building would be filled with darkness.

The darkness is the evidence that there is no light (power source) present, but when you have light in your life, it's the proof that you are connected to God, the true source of light for mankind.

Consider this: when you look at a weightlifter, by the expression of his or her body, you will see that they have been spending time with the weights. You don't have to see them working out, you don't have to see them bench pressing, but when you see them, you can tell where they have been spending their time.

So when God says He is life; and that life was the light of men, He's saying when we see people who have light in their life, it reveals they have been spending time with the light.

But John 1:5 also says, "The light shineth in the darkness and darkness comprehended it not." That word comprehend here means to Admit. The darkness would not Admit it needed the Light.

So when we see people who have darkness in their life, they either have not been exposed to the Light or have not admitted they need Light in their life.

But when people discover and admit (comprehend) and receive the light, their lives reflect direction and purpose because they have a meaningful relationship with the Light.

Because their lives are now connected to something greater than themselves, they have *Divine Illumination* in their life, where they can see beyond where they are, into some creative event to come in their future.

John 1:12, "But as many as received him, to them gave the power to become the sons of God, [even] to them that believe on his name."

John 1:13, "Which were born, not of blood, nor of the will of the flesh, nor of the will of man, but of God."

John 1:14, "And the Word was made flesh, and dwelt among us, (and we beheld his glory, the glory as of the only begotten of the Father,) full of grace and truth."

Insight

John 1:12 reveals God's reproductive process because it says as many as received him, to them gave power to become the sons of God, [even] to them that believe on his name:

Like Ezekiel's Wheel in the Middle of a Wheel, with "Revealed Truth" one Word of Truth is always intended to beget another.

When you start dealing with the "Word of God" made Flesh there's something about God's Abiding Character, Attributes, and Ways, that will begin to paint the Image of His Presence on our life, and people who don't know about your prayer life or what church you go to will be able to tell that you have been with the Light. Even though we don't carry a big cross stapled on our chest outwardly we carry a sign written in our spiritual DNA inwardly. Let's take a look at a biblical example of the Word Made Flesh (Luke 1:26–28, 30, 34-38).

Luke 1:26, "And in the sixth month the angel Gabriel was sent from God unto a city of Galilee, named Nazareth"

Luke 1:27, "To a virgin espoused to a man whose name was Joseph, of the house of David; and the virgin's name [was] Mary."

Luke 1:28, "And the angel came in unto her, and said, Hail, [thou that art] highly favoured, the Lord [is] with thee: blessed [art] thou among women."

First of all, note that this is the "Angel of the Lord" Gabriel[10]. His function in the Kingdom of God is to light the candles of men's heart with divine illumination according to the Times, Seasons, and God's will for their life. So it was with this young woman. She was espoused, (engaged), but she had not gotten married yet, she had not slept with a man, and she was a virgin.

Luke 1:30, "And the angel said unto her, Fear not, Mary: for thou hast found favour with God."

Luke 1:31, "And, behold, thou shalt conceive in thy womb, and bring forth a son, and shalt call his name JESUS."

Luke 1:34, "Then said Mary unto the angel, How shall this be, seeing I know not a man?"

---

[10] Gabriel—champion of God used as a proper name to designate the angel who was sent to Daniel (Dan 8:16), to explain the vision of the ram and the he-goat and to communicate the prediction of the seventy weeks (Dan 9:21–27). He announced also the birth of John the Baptist (Luke 1:11), and of the Messiah (Luke1:26). He describes himself in the words, "I am Gabriel, who stand in the presence of God" (Luke1:19).

Luke 1:35, "And the angel answered and said unto her, The Holy Ghost shall come upon thee, and the power of the Highest shall overshadow thee: therefore also that holy thing which shall be born of thee shall be called the Son of God."

Luke 1:36, "And, behold, thy cousin Elisabeth, she hath also conceived a son in her old age: and this is the sixth month with her, who was called barren."

Luke 1:37, "For with God nothing shall be impossible."

Gabriel tells Mary in Luke 1:31, "You will conceive and bring forth a child and call his name Jesus." What God would place inside of this young virgin was the Word of God figuratively and literally.

Her response is: "How shall this be, seeing I know not a man? Gabriel edifies (strengthens) Mary by telling her that he's "going to connect her with a confirming Word." I'm going to have somebody of like spirit (Like Image) to help you in the *becoming* that God is bringing into your life. *God will always provide confirmation for the Word He is performing in our life.*

Luke 1:36 says, "Your cousin Elizabeth, this is the sixth month with her, who was called barren."

Elizabeth was called Barren because she was unable to have a child on her own until Gabriel came and placed God's Word inside of her (Luke 1:5–13).

So in essence what Gabriel is saying to Mary is you have to press your way upward; you have to go to Elizabeth in Judah (an uphill journey) because I'm going to add strength to your understanding with the witness of a confirming Word (Truth begets Truth).

When we talk about the Word Made Flesh we're speaking of the word being engrafted to our inner man. My prayer is that the things we are sharing now will offer some confirmation that you're on the right path for your life, and the Word that your hearing would become a part of your being, a living thing inside of you.

God gives us confirmation. Because the spirit of man is the candle of the Lord[11], when God illuminates our spirit with revelation or new knowledge, God is faithful to His Word and wants it to prosper inside of us, so He gives us confirmation. Also, God wants man to be After His Likeness, a shadow of His thoughts and movement.

When God confirms His Word, He's exercising the principle of Double Enunciation (saying a thing twice), to establish in earth what has already been established in heaven. In the Word of God when something is done or spoken twice, God is establishing that thing in our heart.

> Gen 41:32 KJV, "And for that the dream was doubled unto Pharaoh twice; [it is] because the thing [is] established by God, and God will shortly bring it to pass."

In Genesis 41:32 we see in Joseph's interpretation of Pharaoh's dreams, that the things of God are confirmed by two or three witnesses. So God is going to send you a witness for the thing that you're becoming, to let you know it's all right to go forward. He tells us it is all right to continue because every promise will be faced with challenges and opposition.

When God reveals His Word to us individually, what He's communicating to us is our prophetic destiny.

Sometimes it will get to the point where it's going to be hard to explain. As it was for Mary, she has a challenge! She had never been with a man and was about to get married! She could not share this with anyone, except Elizabeth because she was having a like experience with God. Even God Himself had to speak to Joseph, Mary's soon to be husband, instructing him to "not put her away (divorce her)," but to keep walking it out, and God Himself was going to

---

[11] Proverbs 20:27: "The spirit of man [is] the candle of the LORD, searching all the inward parts of the belly."

make things work out. So we see that confirmation is important. In Luke 1:37–38, we read:

> Luke 1:37, "For with God nothing shall be impossible[12]."
>
> Luke 1:38, "And Mary said, Behold the handmaid of the Lord; **be it unto me according to thy word**. And the angel departed from her."

How Mary responds is what we have to remember for our self, "Be it unto me according to thy word."

When we receive our Word, our first commission should be to come into agreement with the "Word of God" and acknowledge the Lord's revelation, by telling Him "Let it be unto me according to what you have said. In spite of our circumstances, in spite of not having the tuition for college (provision), in spite of not having a mother or a father in my life (the support I desire), in spite of my life not looking like what God is speaking into my life at the moment I hear it, let it be unto me, according to what your **Word** has said."

Let's look at Ephesians 5. I want to make the distinction that use of **"Word"** in Luke 1:38 is referring to the truth, revealed by His Spirit. In Ephesians 5: 25–26, you will find these Words:

> Eph. 5:25, "Husbands, love your wives, even as Christ also loved the church, and gave himself for it."
>
> Eph. 5:26, "That he might sanctify and cleanse it with the washing of water by the word[13]."

---

[12] (*PAS*[G3956]), In the Greek, it implies *all things* are possible for the individual within the whole and to all individuals in their totally.

[13] Rhema: That which is or has been uttered by the ([1]a) living voice, a thing spoken, an uttered truth. **(Strong's G4487–*rhēma*), ([1]Added for Emphasis).**

Ephesians Chapter 5 starts talking about husbands, wives, and children, and in verse 25, it says, "Husbands love your wives as Christ also loves his church and *gave Himself for it.*"

The reason Christ gave himself for the church is in Eph. 5:26, "That He might sanctify it (set it apart) and cleanse it, with the washing of water by the **Word**."

This is the reason Jesus gave himself to be crucified, buried, and resurrected. So that He might ascend unto heaven as Christ (the Anointed One and His Anointing) and in turn sends His Holy Spirit, so He could reveal who He is in our life, by his **Word**.

If you look at the application of the use "**Word**' in a concordance, in both instances Ephesians 5:26 and in Mary's story in Luke 1:38 where it says "be it unto me according to thy **Word**[14]," it was making reference to Rhema, the revealed word of God, versus Logos[15] (the written word of God).

Mary tells God in Luke 1:38, "Let it be unto your handmaid as the "Word" you have revealed to me." In other words she was saying I receive your Word in spite of my circumstances. I know I'm not married, and this is going to be controversial, but let it be unto me as you have said."

Eph. 5:26 also let us know that we are sanctified (set apart or set in a place of preferred use) and cleansed as the Word becomes manifest in us. The only thing that will cleanse and sanctify us according to our purpose and our destiny is <u>the Word made flesh inside of us.</u>

We are washed with the watering of (the Spirit) by the Word, but we are washed from the inside out, not outside in. The Word becomes hyssop[16] inside of us, as we take possession of the truth

---

[15] See also John 15:3, "*Now ye are clean through the word which I have spoken unto you*". Here the "Word" refers to (Strong's G3056—*logos*) or the spoken then writ-ten word.

[16] (Strong's H231–*ā·zōve*) a plant used for medicinal and religious purposes, As in Psalms 51:7 KJV "*Purge me with hyssop, and I shall be clean: wash me, and I shall be whiter than snow*".

of *who* we are in the Spirit and fulfill the desire of God as it says in Psalms 51:6.

Psalm 51:6, "Behold, thou desirest truth in the inward parts: and in the hidden [part] thou shalt make me to know wisdom."

We met a young lady who said she was called to education. That was her calling. She didn't know why, she didn't understand it when she first began to do it, but she was called to educate people in church about certain things pertaining to raising children. That was her Word. It wasn't in the Bible, but it's what she had been sanctified to do, and she was washed by that. When we are washed, we're washed by the watering (outpouring of the Spirit) over our "Word", the revealed "Truth" inside of us, its purpose and its destiny will always stand in agreement with the Logos or written Word of God.

Destiny Keys and Insights

🔑 When we talk about "The Word Made Flesh" it speaks to two points, the first being Jesus Humanity, a specific point in time when he walked the earth, a window of opportunity for us to witness what God intended for man,

🔑 When the "Word is Made Flesh" there's something about God's Abiding Character, Attributes, and Ways, that will began to paint the Image of His Presence on our life and people who don't know about our prayer life or what church we go to, will be able to tell that you have been with the Him.

My Keys

🔑 _____

🔑 _____

My Insights and Notes

_____
_____
_____
_____
_____
_____
_____
_____
_____
_____
_____
_____
_____
_____

Chapter 4

Not Alone and Not without a Struggle

We have been laying the foundation for the "The Keys to Our Destiny," and so far we have looked at our "Inner Man" (or the inner court of our being). This is God's workshop! It's where He does His work in us. According to Psalms 51:6, it's the place where He desires to hide His truth and for us to have fellowship with His Most Holy Presence. In His objective to save our soul, He sealed the hidden part of us with His Spirit, to counter the effects of what impacts the exposed or outward part of our life.

We also discussed "The Word Made Flesh", which is God's Perspective established in our relationship with Him through our "Inner Man". God's identity is created by our submission to Him and is "projected" onto our "Outer Man", as the "Image of God in our Life".

It is from the projection of God's image that we begin to look at the next dimension of our walk toward destiny: Our Attachments and Our Relationships, but let me begin this conversation by saying when it comes to your success in the progression and ultimate possession of your destiny, *"It's not going to happen through You Alone,"* and *"It's not going to Happen without a Struggle"* in our human nature and what we encounter.

As a point of observation, God did not trust His treasure to our natural mind—He hid it in the spiritual understanding of our hearts, or the Inner Court of our spiritual nature.

Hebrews 8:10 says, "For this [is] the covenant that I will make with the house of Israel after those days, saith the Lord; I will put my laws into their Mind[17], and write them in their hearts[18]: and I will be to them a God, and they shall be to me a people."

Everything we experience in life, everything we perform and every accomplishment must happen at least three times, first in our heart; second in our mind; and third in our actions. These impulses flow throughout our bodies from our hearts and minds faster than 260 mph, so fast that they seem almost seamless, but they are in fact separate cognitive functions.

We must also remember that our natural mind is the receptor and source of expression for all the information and emotions that we have ever encountered, and at times without any voluntary action of our own, premeditation or solicitation, the natural mind can and will recall things from our distant past or present circumstances and bring them forth, imposing those impressions on our present thought-life, including the <u>emotions and will</u> associated with them. Only by the intervention of the Holy Spirit can the emotions and impulses associated with these things imbedded in our soul be brought under subjection to God. Left unguarded or un-renewed in the Spirit, the natural mind can be the cause of much discomfort.

More significant to our purpose and destiny God hides and in many cases has already hidden the treasures of His knowledge in our hearts (not our Soul), and when God wants to do something new with us or raise up a New Thing within us, He quickens that Thing in our heart, New to us, but already known to God.

It is because of this that we must be divinely guided in our human encounters and relationships. They must be orchestrated and ordained by God, so that who walks alone side of us, is aligned with the one who dwells inside of us. This does not mean that every

---

[17] The word Mind in this text means the "Spirit way of thinking and feeling; it implies the *Mind of the Spirit.*"

[18] The Heart; is the fountain and the seat of our thoughts, passions, desires, appetites, affections, purposes, endeavors. Proverbs 4:23 KJV, "Keep thy heart with all diligence; for out of it [are] the issues (forces) of life."

encounter and relationship will be without controversy, but good, bad or indifferent they can all have a meaningful and positive impact on who we are becoming in God.

In the book of Deuteronomy, it says, "His doctrine falls as dew upon a tender herb and then as showers upon the grass[19]."

Ultimately it will pour forth upon us as Rain upon the earth. God's Word is so powerful, when He first reveals His truth to us, He releases it unto us in the very tender knowing of a "Still Small Voice" in our inner man. God will very rarely shock (overwhelm) us with the revelation of who we are, but will often sow it in us, in smallness **(as a seed)** and grow it in us with an unfolding in our understanding, until we would ultimately become what He has revealed.

Looking again at our image—when God said, "Let us make man in our image[20]." What He wants is to be able to hold you up before "His Presence" and see His attributes in you. Man is God's mirror! Also when God wants to display His Glory in the earth, one way that He reveals that glory is through the image He has created in us.

This is such an incredible thing, that even the angels begin to question, "What is man that Thou are mindful of him? Or the son of man that You made him a little bit lower than the angels[21]? In other

---

[19] Deuteronomy *32:2 KJV:* "My doctrine shall drop as the rain, my speech shall distil as the dew, as the small rain upon the tender herb, and as the showers upon the grass."

[20] *Genesis 1:26: The history of creation* (vv. 1–31; cf. Gen 2:4–9; Job 38:4–11; John 1:1–5)

Genesis 1:26 KJV: "And God said, 'Let us make man in our image, after our likeness: and let them have dominion over the fish of the sea, and over the fowl of the air, and over the cattle, and over all the earth, and over every creeping thing that creepeth upon the earth'."

[21] *Psalms 8:4 KJV: The glory of the Lord in Creation* (vv. 1–9; cf. 1 Cor. 15:27; Eph 1:22, 23; Heb. 2:6–8.) *To the Chief Musician, On the instrument of Gath: A Psalm of David.*

Psalms 8:4 KJV: "What is man, that thou art mindful of him? and the son of man, that thou visitest him?"

Psalms 8:5 KJV: "For thou hast made him a little lower than the angels, and hast crowned him with glory and honor."

words, look what God did with the dust!" God's image on our life is an important part of our spiritual life and destiny.

Even in the world we live in today, a lot of the challenges people are going through is about the way their image is cast, how you project and how you carry yourself or whether or not you've got swagger or the "It" factor. This is all about image.

But we must focus on the significance of our image from a spiritual perspective because you only get one chance to make a first impression, and in most cases you get few opportunities in life to display who you really are, especially when you're in the presence of people of importance or in situations of significance. This is not necessarily to impress people, but to accomplish God's will for your life in that moment—your image is very important to your destiny.

The wonderful news is that our God, by His Manifested Glory in our life, is able to manage our image in our encounters and relationships. I know He does this because I have been going through horrific circumstances in my personal life, and nobody else could tell because the presence of God was reigning in my image. We could have a pile of bills, lay-off slips, difficulty with the children, death in the family, bad news from home or trouble with the car.

These circumstances that could take the breath out of us, but by His Grace, we're still able to do our job, fulfill our responsibilities as parents, husbands and wives, and do all the things that we need to do in our life.

Because God is enabling us through the projection of His image in our life, we have Joy in Sadness, Courage in Defeat, and True Humility in our Greatest Triumphs.

There's another side to this wisdom because we never know what the people we encounter are going through in their own life or the significance we're going to play in the day or the season they're experiencing. When they tell us their story, about their morning, or how things are just not working out for them, it should ignite praise in our heart because they felt like they could talk to us, and God trusted us enough to bring them across our path to encourage them, even though we may be feeling pressed beyond measure in our own circumstances.

By God's Grace, we're still able to offer encouragement to friends and strangers, still able to go to work and not look disfigured because God is projecting Himself through our image.

<u>So, if you ever want to look good, I mean, really look good,</u> you need to have God's hands on the Image of your life. I'm not saying that He's going to have you looking like Cleopatra, Beyoncé, Denzel Washington, or Tom Cruise every day of your life, but I can tell you that God can make you look good, even though the times you're going through are difficult and not just make you look good, but cause you to perform with excellence while you're going through what you're experiencing. It's all about image, and God is able to reflect the glory of His Image on the canvas of our humanity.

This is God's Providential and Protective hand, guiding, leading, and sometimes even carrying us through our circumstances. He takes us through life's-challenging encounters, key relationships, and divine appointments, He has chosen for us according to the Purpose, Desire, and Treasure He has hidden in our hearts because "it's not going to happen through you alone" and "it's not going to happen without a struggle." This brings us to the next Key on the road to our Destiny—our "Attachments and Relationships"

Destiny Keys and Insights

God's identity is projected through us by our submission to Him and is "projected from our Inner-Man onto our Outer Man" by the Image of God on our Life.

God hides and in many cases has already hidden the treasures of His knowledge in our hearts (Not our Soul) and when God wants to do something new with us or raise up a New Thing within us, He quickens that "Thing" in our heart, New to Us, but always known to God.

My Keys

_____

_____

My Insights and Notes

_____
_____
_____
_____
_____
_____
_____
_____
_____
_____
_____
_____
_____
_____
_____

Chapter 5

Your Attachments and Relationships

I was talking with my mother some time ago, and believe me, a lot of the things that I'm sharing with you now, I actually heard from my mother first. We were talking, and she was asking me about something that was going on with one of our family member's children. Then she turned to me and said, "Yeah baby, you know, if the devil can't get to you, he'll try to get to you through your children." Those words just rang so true in my spirit and brought to my remembrance the strategically designed attack by the enemy on Job's children[22].

When I first began to receive the wisdom and revelation for "Attachments and Relationships," God dropped into my spirit that "If the devil can't turn you, he will try to turn you by what you love." He'll try to turn you by what your heart is tied to. Let me also add a positive perspective to this. It's a good thing to have affections and attachments in our life, and many times these relationships can serve as early indicators that our times have entered into a new season of change.

I say this knowing that our foundational relationships, such as family, marriage, and children carry over throughout our seasons, but

---

[22] Job 1:18–19, "18 While he [was] yet speaking, there came also another, and said, Thy sons and thy daughters [were] eating and drinking wine in their eldest brother's house: 19 And, behold, there came a great wind from the wilderness, and smote the four corners of the house, and it fell upon the young men, and they are dead; and I only am escaped alone to tell thee."

from time to time, we have to be able to look at these as well as other key relationships from a spiritual and seasonal point of view.

An example of this fact is there is always point of clarity that I can only come into, when I am sitting on the front porch at my mother's house where I grew up, but with that clarity, I must refrain from being driven by the memorabilia of my past experiences, thought patterns and mindsets; submitting them to the "Place of Truth" that God has me at in the present season. This approach is necessary in order to stay focused and accomplish the destiny requirements that are set before me in my now.

The day before this section was going to be delivered to a class that I was teaching, in prayer, as I was trying to clear up some of my own stuff (this is usually how the "truth comes to light"), "Me dealing with Me," and God brought a Scripture to my mind. Now when I say this, most of us who study scripture have heard it and are going to finish the verse in your mind, before you can finish reading it. "Can two people walk together unless they "Agree", right? Okay, that's what I assumed too.

What that Scripture in Amos 3:3 says is *Can two walk together, except they be agreed*[23]. In order to get to the wisdom of agreement, I want to share with you the understanding of the phrase *"except they be agreed"* and add to that, the knowledge of the *Agreed Place*.

---

[23] Agreed: to fix or set. To appoint, assign, designate or betroth; to gather or assemble by appointment.

Wisdom Key

Amos 3:3, "Can two walk together, except they be agreed?"

That word Agreed means "to have been appointed." Can two walk together unless "they have been appointed" or Assigned to each other?

The other thing Agreed implies is to be set in a fixed place or time. Can two walk together unless they are part of the same place, set-time, and season?

Paraphrased: To be "Agreed "is to be "Appointed" or "Assigned" by God for a "Set-Time" and Season".

After receiving this truth regarding Amos 3:3, the Lord really blessed me by opening up my understanding and began to speak to me about God's providential rule over our relationships and how we should be "protecting the Agreed Places" in them.

When I come to that place of clarity sitting on my mother's porch, I didn't move back home because that season in my life is over, and my "Agreed Place" is no longer with my mother at her house, but my agreed place is with my wife, in our home, on my own porch. No matter how much I love my mother or how crazy things can get in my own house with my wife and our circumstances, my "Agreed Place" is with my wife in our home in this season.

At the time of this writing, Charlotte and I have over forty years of marriage, and as I thought about the things that helped us through these many years of marriage, one of them has been that in difficult times we've always been able to find our way back to the "Agreed Place "in the covenant of our marriage.

Now we must understand that in Amos 3:3, God is making a complaint against the children of Israel, because they have gotten off-track again, and the Prophet Amos is chastising them with the Word of the Lord.

God is upset with them because He had already revealed their appointed places, times, and seasons to them, but they have decided to walk contrary to what God has revealed.

They had lost their "Place of Agreement" with God, knowing that God Himself had delivered them and brought them out of Egypt and made them His people; in the beginning they were not a people. They were a man named 'Abraham,' and from the projection of God's image on that one man's life, his son Isaac, and his grandson Jacob, [the son of Isaac, who was later called 'Israel',] and Israel's twelve sons and their decedents, who under the providential care and guidance of God became the children of Israel. After years of God's favored protection and growth, they became the tribes of Israel, He made them a people. They were not a people[24]; **He made them!**

I recapture these facts, to point out the exclusiveness of their "place of agreement" with God. This exclusivity is the same as it is with us today and how we should view God's providential care over us and the influence He allows and brings into our lives through our relationships.

As the redeemed of the Lord, we must understand that He is making us according to his plans for our destiny. God has created and is forming us [Gen 1:26.] Which means He is allowing the right pressure, in the right places, at the right time, with the right relationships, putting the right emphasis upon our thought-life to cause us to become the people that we are in Him.

God has orchestrated our circumstances to get us to the right place and created the atmosphere that would cause us to turn to "Him," hold up our hands and say, "God, I surrender!" God was not amazed on the day you said, "**Jesus, I need you**." And today God is

---

[24] 1 Pet. 2:10 KJV: "Which in time past [were] not a people, but [are] now the people of God: which had not obtained mercy, but now have obtained mercy" (1 Peter 2:10: The chosen stone and His chosen people—vv. 4–10).

saying to us, just like He said to the Children of Israel, that we ought to maintain our "Place of Agreement" in Him.

When the children of Israel had drifted, God sent His Word and said, "Can you continue to walk with Me? Can you find the appointed people I have chosen for your destiny, unless we are agreed?" Unless you're in the appointed time, season, and places that I have prepared for you, can you walk with Me?

God said to me that most of us understand protecting the places of agreement in our natural relationships because when things can go wrong in our relationships with family members, friends or business agreements, we have the conversations, make the necessary apologies or revise the terms of the contract to protect the outcome projected by those places of agreement in the natural.

Insight

Spiritually on the road to destiny, we must understand that many extra-curricular events can happen as well. If we say we're being led by the "Spirit" to Kansas and we become ill or the car breaks down on the way, we have to stay focused on our appointed place. Our destination is Kansas and so concluding the trip in Texas may not be a spiritual option. If Texas has none of appointed time, places or people, it's not the place where we are spiritually agreed. If somehow we get detoured, or something happens, we may end up in Texas, but in order for us to continue to walk in the Spirit we must protect or reconcile the "Agreed Place" with God and in our Spiritual Mind. All other things and places, aside from the place of agreement, no matter how enticing they may be, are just the scenery on the way to the place where the Lord is taking us.

So as I began to look at this, God helped me to understand that as important as this is in our vertical relationship with Him, it also applies to our horizontal relationships with other people. We must not get side tracked, re-directed by our emotions, negative situations or be misguided by out of season relationships or illegal soul ties (unordained covenants).

The Spirit of God is saying there are people He has appointed and set to a fixed place, designated by time, season, and purpose for our lives. Added to this understanding is the knowledge that when God is moving in our lives, we are going to find that our relationships (New and Old) began to take on a greater significance. There is going to come times when God will introduce a significant relationship into our walk with Him and that person or those people have a purpose for a specific time in that season.

Additionally, many of us have experienced relationships where it seems that people, who have been good for us in one season, appear to become contentious in another season. It may not be so much that they have become bad for us, it may just be that the purpose or season for which they were intended has come or is coming to an end. We naturally gravitate toward having friends and people in our life because we need affirmation or just someone to depend on.

Please understand that I too believe in the value of loyalty and that <u>true friendship should be honored</u>. But in the realm of "Spiritual Maturity and Destiny" God continually teaches us that the only person that we can depend upon for our purpose and destiny is Him.

In our human understanding without God's help we would give people a permanent place in our life, when God only intended for them to be there for one chapter or we would give a major part to a person that was only intended to be a role player, according to what God has created us to do.

So when we talk about protecting the places of agreement, <u>the first place of honor and agreement is in our vertical relationship with God</u>; our relationship with God is necessary to receive the flow of the vision for our destiny and the Wisdom and Understanding of the purpose for the season we are experiencing.

Our decisions must be based on what God reveals as we walk with Him. If we betray this knowledge it will set off a domino effect in our life that will require some form of spiritual reconciliation, but I must also add to this, that with God our mistakes (there will be mistakes) are His opportunities, to teach us, prepare us, and show us the magnitude of His Love for us!

As I share with many people that I counsel, I can tell you how you arrived where you are without knowing the details. How So? Because You are where you are because of the decisions we have made; you have arrived at your present state based on your decisions and outside influences, but the good news about that is if a decision and wrong influences got you in trouble, the right decision and right influence can get you out of it. The first decision in times of turmoil should be to turn the situation over to God and "Wait on Him." "Waiting on God" is not being idle; it's doing what He allows and waiting on His next instructions.

The right decisions rest in your vertical relationship with God because God knows **your times, your seasons, and your purpose**. Only God knows that! He has not given the knowledge of these three things to any one individual. He may give your influences a part, but only He knows all three; He didn't even trust it to your own mind. He hid it in your heart. *He gave you the seed of it, so that the fruit of it can come to pass in a season prescribed by Him.*

Many of us who have walked with God are doing things that we never thought we would be doing. If we look at our lives ten years ago, five years ago, or even one year ago for some of us, we never thought it could work out like this! But God set us on a course, and at times introduce new relationships into our life based on the times and the seasons that He knew we would have to endure—it's not by chance. "It's not by power, it's not by might, it's by My Spirit, saith the Lord[25]."

Let me say to some young person or someone who is facing incredible challenges that might be reading this: "Your life has not been left to chance. In this present moment God is *willing* and *able*

---

[25] *Zechariah 4:6 KJV:* vision of the lampstand and olive trees (vv. 1–14).
Zechariah 4:6, Then he answered and spake unto me, saying, "This is the word of the Lord unto Zerubbabel, saying, Not by might, nor by power, but by my spirit, saith the Lord of hosts."

to fulfill and advance the story called 'You,' and guide you back to the Place of Agreement in Him.

God is the narrator of your story, and the "Author and Finisher of Your Faith." So when we talk about maintaining the "Agreed Place," firstly we're talking about our relationship with God, secondarily we must also maintain the horizontal balance of the significant relationships in our lives as well.

Whether those relationships are within our families, business or ministry, they require the covering of our prayer life, so that movement in these strategic positions are based on the revealed will of God.

This must be done, so that we don't lean on our own understanding, operate out of a "Spirit of Error" or make decisions based solely on the difficulty of the surrounding circumstances or our emotions. Our "Agreed Place" must be based on the "Will of God." Or we will end up depending on someone to be something to us that they can't be *or conversely try to be something to somebody that we can't be for them, in the season that they're in.*

Our relationships with the significant people in our lives still come down to understanding Distraction, Deception, and Darkness. If the enemy wants to throw our life off course he must do something to *distract us*, to *deceive us,* or *create a place of darkness that will isolate us* from the light of God. As we stated previously if the enemy can't turn us, he will try to turn us by what we love; what our heart is tied to!

A biblical example of this is Abraham's father Terah. Terah was on his way to Canaan (the Promised Land) and got distracted after the death of his son Haran. Note that he got distracted in a place with the same name of the son he had lost Genesis 11:32 KJV.

Genesis 11:27 KJV, "Now these are the generations of Terah: Terah begat Abram, Nahor, and Haran; and Haran begat Lot."

Genesis 11:28 KJV, "And Haran died before his father Terah in the land of his nativity, in Ur of the Chaldees."

Genesis 11:31 KJV, "And Terah took Abram his son, and Lot the son of Haran his son's son, and Sarai his daughter in law, his son Abram's wife; and they went forth with them from Ur of the Chaldees, to go into the land of Canaan; and they came unto Haran, and dwelt there."

Genesis 11:32 KJV, "And the days of Terah were two hundred and five years: and Terah died in Haran."

Abraham's father, Terah died in Haran, the place where he got distracted. He was supposed to go to what would later be known as the Promised Land that God eventually revealed to Abraham in Genesis 12:5.

Gen 12:5 KJV, "And Abram took Sarai his wife, and Lot his brother's son, and all their substance that they had gathered, and the souls that they had gotten in Haran; and they went forth to go into the land of Canaan; and into the land of Canaan they came."

The Bible says in *Jeremiah 17:9* that "the heart has the potential of the greatest deception, above all things[26]." It says this because the heart is place of your greatest promise, therefore your heart has the potential of your greatest deception; it's the place where God hid the treasure, but if you maintain your heart in the agreed place of God, it will become the place where your greatest victory is birthed.

---

[26] *Jeremiah 17:9 KJV:* Judah's sin and punishment (vv. 1–27)
Jeremiah 17:9, "The heart is deceitful above all things, and desperately wicked: who can know it?"

Destiny Keys and Insights

"If the devil can't turn you, he will try to turn you by what you love."

Amos 3:3 to be "Agreed "is to be "Appointed" or "Assigned" by God for a "Set-Time" or Season."

Our Place of Agreement with God is the exclusivity of His providential care over us and the influence He allows and brings into our lives through our relationships.

God has created and is forming us. [Gen 1:26.] Which means He is allowing the right pressure, in the right places, at the right time, with the right relationships, putting the right emphasis upon our thought-life to cause us to become the people that we are in Him.

My Keys

_____

_____

My Insights and Notes

_____
_____
_____
_____
_____
_____
_____
_____
_____

Chapter 6

Your Destiny: The Will of God

"And we know that all things work together for good
to them that love God, to them who are the called
according to [his] purpose" (Rom 8:28 KJV).

My prayer—my greatest desire—is that the wheels of
your mind and Spirit have begun to catch traction in regards
to your life and your Destiny, that by God's Word and the
help of the Holy Spirit you begin to dig into your purpose and
get the revelation of His will for your life. Just know that
whatever you've done, whatever you've been through, or
wherever state you presently find yourself, God knows where
you're at, and it's not too late! You may have shocked your
parents, your friends, your ex-wife/husband or your
children, by the things that you've done, but God is not
shocked! He knows exactly what you've been through,
exactly what you have experienced, and exactly where you are
today. The Good News is your destiny is waiting on you!
And ready to be fulfilled.

Purpose is everything that God has ordained for us to perform in the
various *Times and Seasons* of our life. Our purpose evolves as we transition through life. *It's the performance of these purposes that acquires
the realm of our destiny.*

Destiny is the summation of those purposes, based on a succession of journeys that cumulates in an ultimate journey (i.e., destiny). Destiny is not a destination that we walk into; Destiny is a realm that we have been prepared to occupy and influence it for the glory of God. *It's what He had in mind when he created us.*

As an example, there was a season when my purpose was fulfilled as a son in my mother's house. I am still a son of that house, but because I have also fulfilled my purpose as a father and a minister in other seasons, when I go home to eulogize a family member and I stand before my family, I stand as a minister to my mother and my family. When we return to my mother's house with the family, I sit at the kitchen table as a son of my mother's house, a minister to my family, and a father to my children. To serve the purpose of my realm in that moment, I must flow effectively between the purposes of a Son, a Minister and a Father.

In this broader understanding of purpose, to be effective in the realm of our destiny, at times we must flow in and out of the knowledge gained in the previous purposes of our life in order to fulfill the ultimate purpose required by our **Destiny.**

We see this in *Psalm 139*, a psalm of David concerning the rebirth of Israel under his Kingship into a new level of hope and the restoration of God's plan for His Kingdom. In verse 17[27], David reflects on his journey and writes concerning the treasure of the Lord's thoughts to him concerning his purpose and destiny. He then speaks to the greatness of the Sum of those thoughts that have been revealed to him[28].

"Real truth begets truth," and every purpose fulfilled will not only gain entry into the next level of purpose, but faithfulness to that "Truth" purchases the sum (*highest view*) of past experiences as we flow into the realm of our destiny. From Psalms 139, we see that David, who was a part of God's Kingdom strategy, had the thoughts

---

[27] Psalms 139:17 KJV: "How precious also are thy thoughts unto me, O God! How great is the [27]sum of them!"

[28] *Ro'sh* H7218: The Head; the best, whatever is highest and supreme (i.e., the highest or best view of a thing).

of God! God also showed His Ways to Moses[29] and even though "His Thoughts and Ways may be pass finding out," according to Romans 11:33; they are revealed to those who seek Him.

When we read Isaiah 55:8, where it says, "For my thoughts are not your thoughts, neither are your ways my ways, saith the LORD;" Many have concluded from this verse, that God will not share His thoughts and ways with us, *but this is far from the truth.*

Because when we look at Isaiah 55:8, in context of Isaiah 55:7 where it says, "*Let the wicked forsake his way, and the unrighteous man his thoughts[30],*" we see that in Isaiah 55:8 he was speaking in reference to the "*Wicked and Unrighteous*" forsaking their thoughts and ways for the Thoughts and Ways of God.

Also Isaiah 55: 10–11 *goes on to say that "as the rain comes from above, and the snow from heaven, and cause the earth to bud and prosper ... so shall my Word (thoughts) be that goes forth out of my mouth and it shall prosper in the thing to which I send it—it shall not come back to Me barren"* (paraphrased).

Jesus, our example would also say in the New Testament, "I don't do anything unless My Father tells me[31]," a speaking Father to

---

[29] Psalms 103:7 KJV: "He made known his ways unto Moses, his acts unto the children of Israel."

[30] *Isaiah 55:7–11 KJV*—an invitation to abundant life (context vv. 1–13):

7 Let the wicked forsake his way, and the unrighteous man his thoughts: and let him return unto the LORD, and he will have mercy upon him; and to our God, for he will abundantly pardon.

8 For my thoughts are not your thoughts, neither are your ways my ways, saith the LORD.

9 For as the heavens are higher than the earth, so are my ways higher than your ways, and my thoughts than your thoughts.

10 For as the rain cometh down, and the snow from heaven, and returneth not thither, but watereth the earth, and maketh it bring forth and bud, that it may give seed to the sower, and bread to the eater:

11 So shall my word be that goeth forth out of my mouth: it shall not return unto me void, but it shall accomplish that which I please, and it shall prosper in the thing whereto I sent it.

[31] *John 8:28 KJV:* Jesus predicts His departure (context vv. 21–30). "Then said Jesus unto them, When ye have lifted up the Son of man, then shall ye know that

a hearing Son. The path to our destiny is not only known by God, but His thoughts are revealed to us by His Spirit and to those He has choose to speak into our lives or confirm our journeys.

God knows the places, times, and seasons where you will experience your victories, struggles, and challenges, and He is willing to share His Thoughts, Plans, and Strategies with those that seek Him.

Paul instructs the church, on one occasion about *Praying in Your Most Holy Prayer.* What he's asking us to do, is not just to pray in the Spirit (the gift), but he is instructing us 'that we should pray under the (presence) and Power of the Holy Spirit, that moved at creation in the beginning, because by the Holy Spirit we gain access to the plan that God has for us.' We should trust no other relationship above the relationship that we have with God through the Holy Spirit.

He put His Spirit in our life the day that we got saved. The day you got saved, you were sealed with Holy Spirit![32] The Holy Spirit reconnected you with the purpose and ultimate destiny God planned for your life before you were even in your mother's womb[33]. The Holy Spirit is the only one who absolutely knows who you are in God.

The first thing we need to understand about "**Destiny**" is that Everybody has one. Not one of us has been left out of God's will. We are all intended to perform at some level in the Holy Spirit to manifest His Kingdom in the earth and accomplish the things He has ordained for us to perform.

God's Grace often comes as divine enablement; this is the ability for us to perform the things that He wants us to perform, often while surviving opposition and overcoming obstacles in the season that we are in.

I am he, *and that I do nothing of myself; but as my Father hath taught me, I speak these things."*

[32] 2 Co. 1:22 KJV: "Who hath also sealed us, and given the earnest of the Spirit in our hearts" (Also see Ephesians 4:30).

[33] Jeremiah 1:5 KJV: "Before I formed thee in the belly I knew thee; and before thou camest forth out of the womb I sanctified thee, [and] I ordained thee a prophet unto the nations."

You may not be flowing in the Grace of your destiny right now or you may be in a season of waiting (Preparation), and it seems like things are on hold, but waiting is not a bad thing, because purpose takes patience and waiting is one of God's strategies to perfect His timing.

The second thing we need to understand about "**Destiny**" is the purpose of our destiny is to leave a legacy. As we gain influence in our realm for the reign and the rule of God, we are also positioned to impact the legacy for our generations. As we look at the lives and destinies of God's people (Abraham, Joseph, Moses, Esther, Ruth, and David) just to mention a few, we see a similar pattern; their lives consisted of a series of journeys and on each leg of their journey, their lives became more Influential and more Generational in impact.

The fullness may take years to manifest, but it's the journey itself that propels the destiny and the performance of purpose that defines it. As God illuminates, who you are, He increases the impact of your influence and the things that you do best; this creates a definitive awareness of the gifts, talents and anointing, He has deposited in your life.

The third and probably the most important thing we need to understand is that our Destiny is tied to the legacy of Jesus the Christ which is "The Kingdom of God" in the earth.

If you look at the pattern in Jesus life, at birth He was on a journey because He had to leave Bethlehem and go to Egypt, to escape the murderous plot of Herod (The Flight into Egypt—Matt 2:13–16). That was followed by many sub-journeys, including the one to the Jordan River for His baptism, where afterward He was led into the wilderness by the Spirit for forty days of testing; <u>tests often precede a new level or season.</u>

After this sequence of events, His first order of business was the Gospel of the Kingdom[34], followed by the Gospel of Salvation as a requirement for entering the Kingdom of God. When Jesus's disciples asked Him how to pray, His instructions included praying for

---

[34] Mark 1:15 KJV: "And saying, The time is fulfilled, and the kingdom of God is at hand: repent ye, and believe the gospel."

"His Kingdom to be fulfilled in earth as it is in heaven[35]," and that prayer closed with the words *"Thine is the Kingdom the Power and the Glory."* Of course, we know that His ultimate journey was to the Cross, where He delivered us from sin. Amen! It was at the cross that our destiny became a part of His legacy, the kingdom of God.

From the life of Jesus the Christ, those who preceded Him and we who follow after Him, we see that Destiny is a series of journeys that cumulates in an ultimate journey that carries forth the "Purpose, Glory, and Will of the Father and His Kingdom.

Destiny is not a destination; it is a realm of influence that you acquire by God pouring Himself through your life. As that realm expands, it becomes the ultimate evangelism, 'You' influencing the earth realm on God's behalf.

---

[35] Mat. 6:9 KJV: "After this manner therefore pray ye: Our Father which art in heaven, Hallowed be thy name."

Mat. 6:10 KJV: "Thy kingdom come. Thy will be done in earth, as [it is] in heaven."

Mat. 6:13 KJV: "And lead us not into temptation, but deliver us from evil: For thine is the kingdom, and the power, and the glory, forever. Amen."

Destiny Key

When we speak of Destiny as a series of journeys, we must realize that the very nature of a journey is leaving a present experience for something that may or may not be fully known or understood. Also a journey is not always leaving something that is necessarily bad, but often times, it's leaving something that was good, for something that is greater.

Many people don't engage the Kingdom of God because of the challenge to the comfort zone of their present mind-set. They don't want to risk the Spiritual Experience at the present level of knowledge they have, in order to gain "New Knowledge" in another realm.

And because they won't let go of what's in their hands, they deny themselves access to the Secret things of God Revealed by His Spirit. This is what you see in "traditional thought" or "rehearsed behavior." In the church, there are those who are reluctant sojourners who want things to remain the same. They want the choir to sing the same songs, they want to be able to sit in their same pew, and let me be clear, there's nothing wrong with the songs or sitting in the same pews. It's the Mind Set behind the action that minimizes the experience of God's Kingdom.

Mind Sets are thought patterns that have been established in our mind over time, something that we defend, in our heart; A Stronghold has to do with our will and is tied to an emotion from a former action that is based on what's going on inside our heart[36]. *Mindsets and Strongholds support each other*: If I say in my heart that, 'I'm better than my neighbor,' my mind-set says

---

[36] 2 Corinthians 10:4–5 KJV: "4 (For the weapons of our warfare [are] not carnal, but mighty through God to the pulling down of strong holds;) 5 Casting down imaginations, and every high thing that exalteth itself against the knowledge of God, and bringing into captivity every thought to the obedience of Christ."

'put up a fence'. So I put these barriers up between my neighbor and me, between their children and my children! I won't let them in, but I can't get out. It's a Stronghold! So we have to be careful of 'mind-sets, strongholds, and things of the flesh that will hold us back from the "Kingdom and our Destiny." What we want for our destiny is not our thoughts; what we want is the *mind of Christ* the King of the Kingdom.

One of the first keys to proceeding into our destiny and the Kingdom is to be transformed by the renewing of our minds [*Rom 12:1–2 NKJV: Living Sacrifices to God*].

By the Mind of Christ we receive an impartation of His thoughts into our thought-life, which carries us beyond our present state of thought and understanding, correcting and instructing us in the plans and strategies of God. (With this new knowledge of his kingdom, we receive Revelation Knowledge and Vision).

By the[37] Mind of His Spirit, inside of us there's a quickening of the His Spirit in the thoughts we have received by revelation. (As we walk in the quickening of this renewed thought life; we receive Guidance).

By this relationship with Christ in the Sprit realm we can discern a Mind-Set, or fixation upon something, that is not subject to the will of God or when we are being ruled over by a Stronghold, which is the subjection of our will to a thought that does not rest under the captivity of the Holy Spirit.

The Bible says, "lean not unto your own understanding, but acknowledge God in all your ways and he shall direct thy paths[38]."

---

[37] Rom. 8:26–27 KJV: "26 Likewise the Spirit also helpeth our infirmities: for we know not what we should pray for as we ought: but the Spirit itself maketh intercession for us with groanings which cannot be uttered. 27And he that searcheth the hearts (Christ), knoweth what [is] the mind of the Spirit, because he maketh intercession for the saints according to [the will of] God."

[38] *Proverbs 3:5-6 KJV:* Guidance for the young (vv. 1–35), "5 Trust in the LORD WITH all thine heart; and lean not unto thine own understanding. 6 In all thy ways acknowledge him, and he shall direct thy paths."

Destiny Keys and Insights

Purpose is everything that God has ordained for us to perform in the various *Times and Seasons* of our life.

Destiny is not a destination that we walk into; destiny is a realm that we have been prepared to occupy by the purposes we have fulfilled and influence for the glory of God.

The first thing we need to understand about "Destiny" is that "Everybody Has One." Not one of us has been left out of God's will.

When we speak of Destiny as a series of journeys, we must realize that the very nature of a journey is leaving a present experience for something that may or may not be fully known or understood.

My Keys

_____

_____

My Insights and Notes

_____
_____
_____
_____
_____
_____
_____
_____

Chapter 7

Spiritual Transition

In summary of our definition for **Destiny;** as the summation of purposes, performed in a succession of journeys, that cumulate in an "Ultimate Journey". We must consider that in the true nature of a journey, in the pursuit of our destiny we will experience "**Transition**".

When we speak of transition in spiritual terms, it is not merely moving from one place to another location. In the realm of destiny, Transition is a spiritual transaction that acquires a Higher Level of Influence, Greater Authority, Enlarged Territories or some New Beginning. Transitions often bear the fruit of a clearer perspective of God's plan for us and a broader understanding of our life's preceding events and purposes.

In the book of Ruth, its (presumed) author, the Prophet Samuel, uses four chapters and just eighty-five verses to concisely present the transition of Ruth the Moabites, from Moab to Bethlehem-Judah. Ruth enters Bethlehem as a gleaner of leftovers in the fields of harvest and transitions into the wife of Boaz, a Jewish socialite in Bethlehem and forerunner in the bloodline of Jesus Christ.

Prophet Samuel not only details Ruth's transition, but the book of Ruth also traces the transition of the Jewish Nation from the times of Judges[39] before the Book of Ruth to the time of Kings[40] that follow in the book of I Samuel; ultimately pointing to the anointing of David as King and predecessor to Christ.

Because Prophet Samuel is its author, the Book of Ruth is filled with prophetic insight and spiritual understanding for us as we go through our own transitions. Remember we go through transition; it is a temporary state that produces lasting and positive change in the lives of those who persevere. To the natural eye <u>Transition</u> will often appear as though we are in trouble, but the spiritual reality is that we are just in transition to another place in God.

And so it appears in the story of Ruth;

> **Ruth 1:3 KJV**—And Elimelech Naomi's husband died; and she was left, and her two sons.
>
> **Ruth 1:5 KJV**—And Mahlon and Chilion died also both of them; and the woman was left of her two sons and her husband.

When Ruth's husband, her Father in-law and brother in-law die, it is a true tragedy, but not the death of Ruth's destiny; She is evangelized, by her mother-in-law Naomi and finds purpose in her pain. She has not begun her transition, but her transition occurs when she comes to the place where she makes a decision.

> **Ruth 1:15 KJV**—And she (Naomi) said, **Behold, thy sister in law is gone back unto her people**, and unto her gods: return thou after thy sister in law.

---

[39] Ruth 1:1 KJV—Now it came to pass in the days when the judges ruled, that there was a famine in the land. And a certain man of Bethlehem-Judah went to sojourn in the country of Moab, he, and his wife, and his two sons. Ruth 1:2 KJV—And the name of the man [was] Elimelech, and the name of his wife Naomi, and the name of his two sons Mahlon and Chilion, Ephrathites of Bethlehem-Judah. And they came into the country of Moab, and continued there.

[40] 1Samuel 16:13 KJV—Then Samuel took the horn of oil, and anointed him in the midst of his brethren: and the Spirit of the LORD came upon David from that day forward. So Samuel rose up, and went to Ramah.

> **Ruth 1:16 KJV**—And Ruth said, Intreat me not to leave thee, [or] to return from following after thee: for whither thou goest, I will go; and where thou lodgest, I will lodge: thy people [shall be] my people, and thy God my God:

Oprah chooses to remain in Moab, but Ruth makes a decision that changes the course of her life. Rather than conform to the circumstances of the place that she is in; Ruth decides to follow after her hope in the God she has come to know through her mother-in-law Naomi. Spiritual Transition is never left to a Choice, because Destiny requires the commitment of a Decision.

> Ruth 1:22 KJV—So Naomi returned, and Ruth the Moabitess, her daughter in law, with her, which returned out of the country of Moab: **and they came to Bethlehem in the beginning of barley harvest.**

Here Naomi is a type of the Holy Spirit who comes along side of Ruth, meeting her where she is and leading her to Bethlehem-Judah; the ("House of Bread and Place of Praise").

Ruth's decision not only changes the course of her life, but it brings her into divine alignment with God's purpose and timing. **Transitions that are God initiated,** bring the blessing of His providential care and timing, turning apparent defeat into triumph and carrying us into our highest good.

Ruth and Naomi leave Moab a place of tragedy and devastation and enter Bethlehem at the time of Harvest and increase, but God's divine orchestration continues. When Ruth goes to glean left-overs from the portion of the field that is designated for the poor according to Levitical law. Unknown to her, but orchestrated by God, she is lead to the field that is owned by Boaz. That is miraculous in and of itself, but **Ruth 2:4-5** shows us evidence of two more pieces of God's Providential and Excellent Guidance;

> Ruth 2:4 KJV—And, behold, Boaz came from Bethlehem, and said unto the reapers, The LORD [be] with you. And they answered him, The LORD bless thee.
>
> Ruth 2:5 KJV—Then said Boaz unto his servant that was set over the reapers, whose damsel [is] this?

First Boaz comes from Bethlehem to his field on the day that Ruth Shows up! Secondarily Boaz notices Ruth, out of all the gleaners in the field, **Boaz notices Ruth!**

Life happens to all of us, but God has proved time and time again, that when it comes to your destiny, and God's providential transitions, He not only makes things turn around in your favor, but He takes what looks like it is working against you and makes it work together for your good.

Ruth's transition takes on a new dimension when Boaz speaks to her in **Ruth 2:11**—And Boaz answered and said unto her, **It hath fully been shewed me,** all that thou hast done unto thy mother in law since the death of thine husband: and [how] thou hast left thy father and thy mother, and the land of thy nativity, and art come unto a people which thou knewest not heretofore. (See Mark 10:29-30[41] Below)

Where Boaz says; "It Has Been Fully Shown to Me" he is making reference to the fact that Moabites were disqualified from entering into fellowship with the Israelites because, Balak the son of Zippor, king of Moab, sought Balaam to curse them when they came out of

---

[41] Mark 10:29-30 KJV—And Jesus answered and said, Verily I say unto you, there is no man that hath left house, or brethren, or sisters, or father, or mother, or wife, or children, or lands, for my sake, and the gospel's, Mark 10:30 But he shall receive a hundredfold; now in this time, houses, and brethren, and sisters, and mothers, and children, and lands, with persecutions; and in the world to come eternal life.

Egypt[42], this was decreed in Deuteronomy23:3[43], but Boaz has added spiritual insight and probably also has a place in his heart for Ruth, because of the ridicule that his Grandmother, Rahab the Harlot had received; who also was part of the linage of Jesus Christ, according to Matthew 1;1 and 1:5

> **Matthew 1:1** The book of the generation of Jesus Christ, the son of David, the son of Abraham
>
> **Matthew 1:5**-Salmon the father of Boaz, whose mother was Rahab, Boaz the father of Obed, whose mother was **Ruth**, Obed the father of Jesse **Matthew 1:6A and Jesse begat David the king**;

Boaz in this sense is a type of Christ, as our Savior Jesus who became like us, so He could understand and redeem us; So is Boaz in this instance, being in touch with feelings of Ruth's infirmities, that he knows from his grandmother's experience; and even though the judgement of her past says that Ruth is not qualified; Boaz is uniquely prepared to look past the judgement of the decree and see the plan God in her life.

And instead of judgement, Boaz speaks the **"Promise of Recompense"** over Ruth's life[44]. in Ruth 2:12 KJV—The LORD

---

[42] Numbers 22:9 KJV—And God came unto Balaam, and said, What men [are] these with thee? Numbers 22:10 KJV—And Balaam said unto God, Balak the son of Zippor, king of Moab, hath sent unto me, [saying], Numbers 22:11 KJV—Behold, [there is] a people come out of Egypt, which covereth the face of the earth: come now, curse me them; peradventure I shall be able to overcome them, and drive them out.

[43] Deuteronomy 23:3 KJV—An Ammonite or Moabite shall not enter into the congregation of the LORD; even to their tenth generation shall they not enter into the congregation of the LORD forever:

[44] **Targum from the Dakes Annotated Reference Bible**: Boaz words "it has been certainly told me" (1) (**implies he has been informed**) by the word of the wise what the Lord hath decreed in ((1) **Deuteronomy 23:3**), saying He hath not decreed of this concerning this woman, but those men at that time adding, "**And it has surely been said to me by prophesy, ((1) Probably by the Prophet Samuel),**

recompense thy work, and a full reward be given thee of the LORD God of Israel, under whose wings thou art come to trust. **Two points should be observed:**

- The first is that when you go through transition according to God's purpose, He has people in place the will see you according to the will of God
- The second point is when you come through a spiritual transition, past judgments on your life will not be able to disqualify you.

In **Ruth 2:14** Boaz repositions Ruth with his favor and sits her among the reapers, to share in their portion, which means that she would now reap, what she had not sown.

Ruth 2:14 KJV—And Boaz said unto her, At mealtime come thou hither, and eat of the bread, and dip thy morsel in the vinegar. And she sat beside the reapers: and he reached her parched [corn], and she did eat, and was sufficed, and left.

What takes place next is one of the most powerful transitional steps revealed in Ruth's Journey; when Boaz places purpose in her hands, by commanding the young men that work for him saying in **Ruth 2:16-17**

KJV—And let fall also [some] of the handfuls of purpose for her, and leave [them], that she may glean [them], and rebuke her not. **Ruth 2:17** So she gleaned in the field until even, and beat out that she had gleaned: **and it was about an ephah, or (60LBS) of barley, (A Reapers Portion of Purpose, but not "Destiny" yet).**

What' purpose has God placed in your hands to perform, while you're waiting on your promise to be fulfilled? It may not be something in your hand, it could be a vision in your heart, a witty

---

that kings and prophets shall come out of you, because of the good you have done". (1) **Added for Clarity.**

invention in your mind, a future hope for your children and family. A part time job until full-time employment comes.

How we walk out the present purpose God has given us, will have great influence on how we receive our destiny. How many successful businesses, prosperous ideas, how many children transformed into doctors, top athletes and great leaders coming from the background to the forefront, because they, some mother or spiritually assigned person has persevered in performing the mundane tasks of purpose until something they seen in the spirit comes to past.

In Ruth 2:19 we read—And her mother in law said unto her, where hast thou gleaned to day? and where did you wrought? (paraphrased), blessed be he that did take knowledge of thee. And she shewed her mother in law with whom she had wrought, and said, the man's name with whom I wrought to day [is] Boaz.

The word "**Wrought**" in **Ruth 2:19** has the same meaning as "**Exploits**" in **Dan 11:32** and implies works performed under the **"Power of the Spirit" Dan 11:32B KJV—but the people that do know their God shall be strong, and do [exploits].**

Ruth would be strong and perform her exploits for all of the Barley and Wheat harvest; from Passover to Pentecost and God's plan would take Ruth from the Purpose in her hands to the hope of Destiny that was in her heart. Just think the summation of the purpose that was placed in the hands of Ruth the Moabitess, was the Destiny of the life she would live with Boaz! **Ruth becomes a type of the Church, redeemed by Boaz to be his Bride.**

Keys to Destiny Life from the Inside-Out Manuscript Edits Phase 4

Destiny Keys and Insights

- On the other side of your transition God has established people that will see you according to His Will

- When you come out of your spiritual transition, past judgements on your life will not disqualify you

- No matter how insufficient or how small it may seem, when GOD puts purpose in your hand He has a Promise and a Plan for it!

My Keys

- _____

- _____

My Insights and Notes

_____
_____
_____
_____
_____
_____
_____
_____
_____
_____
_____
_____

Chapter 8

The Kingdom of God

A topic we hear talked about a lot in our churches is the Kingdom of God. Added to this we hear comments like, "They have a Kingdom Ministry," "You have a Kingdom anointing on your life" or "I see that you're walking in the principles of the kingdom." Spiritually we need to be more discerning in what is meant by the Kingdom, so that we can better understand the foundation of where our destiny comes from.

Scripture teaches to us that we should not think of the Kingdom in stagnate terms[45]; or think that the Kingdom is designated for some future time. The present truth is that the Kingdom exists in its present state, inside of us, and we should witness the kingdom coming (*in part*) as it is fulfilled in the members of the "Body of Christ" as we take our destined positions. This with the understanding that in the fullness of time, the Kingdom will (*fully*) manifest, and Christ its King will come and be seated in the earth.

The Kingdom of Heaven is a future destination for believers, and the Kingdom of God is the realm in the earth where God exercises His will. In some cases the Kingdom of God and the Kingdom of Heaven are used interchangeably because God has the Reign,

---

[45] Luke 17:20–21 KJV: "20 And when he was demanded of the Pharisees, when the kingdom of God should come, he answered them and said, The kingdom of God cometh not with observation: 21Neither shall they say, Lo here! or, lo there! for, behold, the kingdom of God is within you."

Rule, and Authority over both, but when we talk about the Kingdom of God, from our present perspective, we're talking about the territory and realm we occupy both spiritually and geographically on His behalf.

The Kingdom of God[46] is the sphere of God's rule, that also includes the people over whom God rules and the territory they occupy. This knowledge is being taught and shared by many ministries, but I want to correlate the Kingdom of God to our destiny.

As citizens of God's earthly kingdom, we receive <u>authority, instructions, and guidance</u>, in the matters of the King, but we also receive vision, revelation, and wisdom for our purpose and destiny that is tied to the legacy of Christ the king of that kingdom.

The Anointing that flows from Christ[47] the Head of the Church fills us with His purposes and solutions for the Kingdoms of this world and positions us into strategic places of influence (dominion) in order to release the answers they require. By the Works of His Spirit, (i.e., Word of Wisdom, Word of Knowledge, and Ability to Discern the Times and Seasons, etc.), the anointing from Christ, the King of Glory[48] is released through us to fulfill our Divine assignments (Destiny) in His kingdom. This activity is orchestrated from the Throne of Christ, who is seated at the "right hand of God the Father in the Kingdom of God[49]. All this is transpiring because of the coming of His Kingdom in the earth, so our understanding of the kingdom's operations is essential to understanding our destiny.

---

[46] *The Kingdom: Basileia, (basileia, NT: 932) is primarily an abstract noun, denoting "sovereignty, royal power, dominion; then, by metonymy, a concrete noun, denoting the territory or people over whom a king rules, e.g., Mt 4:8; Mk 3:24. It is used especially of the "kingdom" of God and of Christ.*

[47] *Christos*: The Anointed one and His Anointing

[48] Psalms 24:10 KJV: "Who is this King of glory? The LORD of hosts, he [is] the King of glory. Selah."

[49] Hebrews 8:1 KJV "Now of the things which we have spoken [this is] the sum: We have such an high priest, who is set on the right hand of the throne of the Majesty in the heavens."

Chapter 9

God's Order

The Power of the kingdom flows through "God's Order." There can be no demonstration of His Power (Authority) without a clear-cut foundation of God's order. In Ephesians chapter 4, the operation of God's order is revealed. Ephesians 4:7 says, "But unto every one of us is given grace according to the measure of the gift of Christ." The entire "Body of Christ" is enabled (Powered By) the measure of His Anointing, but Ephesians 4:11 adds to this, that five dimensions of the Headship of Christ has been delivered to His Body.

> Ephesians 4:11 "And he gave some, apostles; and some, prophets; and some, evangelists; and some, pastors and teachers;[50]"

Those with this Headship Anointing are a gift to the Church from Christ. Their operation in God's Order is essential to the functioning of the Body of Christ and His Kingdom as these five-fold ministers facilitate the callings and destinies of the saints to bring the whole body into a state of fullness, as stated in

> Ephesians 4:13 Till we all come in the unity of the faith, and of the knowledge of the Son of God, unto a perfect man, unto the measure of the stature of the fullness of Christ:

---

[50] See Appendix for further detail of the Gifts to the Body of Christ.

These headship gifts (offices) while specific are not stagnate and can demonstrate some overlap in function, some having a primary office, while also demonstrating a secondary gift (i.e., prophetic pastors, evangelical teachers, etc.). In the times of Paul's introduction of these gifts, some hearers and readers would have had a special insight to their purpose. For instance, Apostles is taken from the word (Apollo) that was recognized by the people of that day as the same name of the lead ship in the Phoenician Navy that operated vast trading networks. They were also known as <u>master navigators, shipbuilders, and craftsmen</u> equipped with the highest skill levels, best plans, and condiments of the king and sent forth with the highest level of authority.

Paul was following this line of thought when he says that as the Lord's apostle he had become a "*Wise Master Builder,*" poised and positioned for dominion in the present state of the Kingdom.

First Corinthians 3:10 "According to the grace of God which is given unto me, as a wise master builder, I have laid the foundation, and another buildeth thereon. But let every man take heed how he buildeth thereupon."

The function of this lead (Apollo's) vessel in the Phoenician Navy was the same as for the Apostles in the Church: to carry all of the significant Messages, Emblems, Flags, and Marks of the King into new territories, including the King's signet Ring that gave the ship (vessel) complete authority to represent the King and his Kingdom, *such as it is with the Anointing that rest on these* five-fold ministry gifts. The aim of this function was to establish the very essence of the of the King's domain, so that when the King came to the claimed territory, He would see the reflections of His Kingdom.

As Christ's believers under this order, we are His Ambassadors[51], His Emissaries, and the possessors of the Glory of His will in the

---

[51] 2 Corinthians 5:20 KJV, "Now then we are ambassadors for Christ, as though God did beseech [you] by us: we pray [you] in Christ's stead, be ye reconciled to God."

earth realm. As ambassadors of Christ our destiny is tied to His "purpose" as we are "the called" according to His purpose (Romans 8:28). The Church rests within the Body of the King and births (Reproduces) the essence of His kingdom, promotes its order (Structure), and carries out its mandates (Territorial Exploits) on behalf of Christ its King. This is to be accomplished to fulfill the scripture that says, *"The kingdoms of this world are become [the kingdoms] of our Lord"* (Rev 11:15).

nation they were destined to become, they must conquer the greatness and might of the nations that were set before them in these seven nations. At the time the word from *Deuteronomy 7:1* was revealed to Moses by the Lord. These seven nations represented the seven major influences in that region of world in Moses lifetime.

In our times, the seven pillars of influence or seven mountains as some refer to them can be summarized as *Religion*[55], *Family, Business, Education, Government, Arts and Entertainment*, and the *Media*. This understanding has been received by many through independent revelations, and the message of these seven pillars of influence has also been carried by many into the Body of Christ on a global level, including Lance Wallnau, Peter Wagner, John Enlow and others.

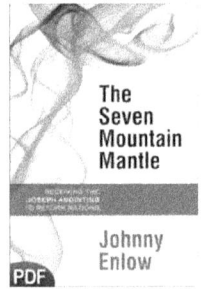

The
Seven
Mountain
Mantle

Johnny
Enlow

Wisdom Key:

This is a present truth of the Kingdoms of this World in our times, but our world is evolving even as we speak. Technology and the Medical Sciences could easily be considered if we take into account their impact on the existing seven pillars of influence as a whole and the influence they currently represent.

---

[55] Religion; here represents the portions of the Church that remain trapped in mindsets and strongholds that hinder its greatness, so this is not Christ opposing His Church, but him delivering his body from the thoughts and ways that oppose His will.

Chapter 11

The Wisdom of God's Kingdom

Proverbs 8:1–3 says, "[8:1]Doth not wisdom cry? And understanding put forth her voice? [8:2] She standeth in the top of high places, by the way in the places of the paths. [8:3] She crieth at the gates, at the entry of the city, at the coming in at the doors."

These verses let us know that Wisdom does cry out and Understanding puts forth her voice! They stand in the top of high places (*mountains*), cry at the gates, and put forth their voice at the entry of the city, at the coming in at the doors. *God's wisdom is best and most heard at the time of our advance unto the high places of this world and at the entering of the gates of new territories and open doors.*

Proverbs 9:1 follows by saying, "Wisdom has built her house. She has hewn out her seven pillars."

These are the words of Solomon who received the wisdom of God and built one of the greatest displays of God's kingdom in the Bible, and now the Lord is releasing His wisdom and the anointing for the establishing of His house on the seven pillars or mountains of this world.

According to Proverbs 24:3–4 KJV: "Through wisdom is an house builded; and by understanding it is established: And by knowledge shall the chambers be filled with all precious and pleasant riches[56]."

---

[56] Wisdom; *Strong's H2451;chokmah*, skilled (in war, administration and spiritual affairs):

Wisdom is the divine application of revealed Knowledge. The knowledge of the seven pillars and its relevance to the Gospel of the Kingdom is the will of God according to His purposes. The advance of this knowledge requires His wisdom in order for it to be fulfilled. *The kingdoms of this world become the kingdoms of our Lord, when the people filled with the "Knowledge of His Will and Wisdom" occupy their Place in the Kingdom.*

In every generation, God has anointed leaders with the vision and wisdom to raise up a people for the advancement of His Kingdom in the earth. For the children of Israel, that leader was Moses, who received the anointing and vision of God from the burning bush experience. There was also David who was anointed by the Lord's prophet Samuel to advance God's kingdom against the Philistines, and there was a host of others including Jesus who said in Luke 4:18 KJV, "The Spirit of the Lord [is] upon me, because he hath anointed me to preach the gospel to the poor; he hath sent me to heal the brokenhearted, to preach deliverance to the captives, and recovering of sight to the blind, to set at liberty them that are bruised."

As it was spoken in the New Testament, so it was prophesized by Isaiah in the Old Testament in Isaiah 61:1[57] KJV, and from these texts we see that the anointing is always for purpose and from the cross of our salvation, our purposes and our destinies are tied to the legacy of *Christ, the Anointed One and His Anointing.*

Understanding; *Strong's H8394*; *tabuwn, divine* insight; (to perceive or discern; the object of knowledge).

Knowledge; *Strong's H3045*; *yada'*, (Qal) to know, (Niphal) to be instructed (Hiphil) to make known, *Strong's H7337*; to be enlarged (Psalms 31:8).

[57] Isa 61:1 KJV: "The Spirit of the Lord GOD [is] upon me; because the LORD hath anointed me to preach good tidings unto the meek; he hath sent me to bind up the brokenhearted, to proclaim liberty to the captives, and the opening of the prison to [them that are] bound."

Appendix

The "Gifts from God the Father" are foundational and serve God's original intent (Rom. 12:2). These are "Inherent Tendencies" (present at birth but not necessarily hereditary) tendencies that characterize each person by reason of the Creator's unique workmanship in their initial gifting that establishes their place in God's created order. While seven categories are listed, observation would reveal that few people are fully described by only one.

Gifts of the Father *Romans 12.3–8: (Foundational for Life and Purpose)*[58]

1. Prophecy
    a. To speak with forthrightness and insight, especially when enabled by the Spirit of God (Joel 2:28).
    b. To demonstrate moral boldness and uncompromising commitment to worthy values.
    c. To influence others in one's arena of influence with a positive spirit of social or spiritual righteousness.

2. Ministry
    a. To minister or a render loving service prompted by the Holy Spirit, general service to meet the needs of others.
    b. Illustrated in the work and office of the deacon (Matt. 20:26).

---

[58] "Holy Spirit Gifts and Power" by Paul Walker, *Spirit filled life study Bible*. 1997, c1991 (electronic ed.) (Re 22:18). Nashville: Thomas Nelson;

3. Teaching
   a. The supernatural ability to explain and apply the truths received from God for the church.
   b. Presupposes study and the Spirit's illumination providing the ability to make divine truth clear to the people of God.
   c. Considered distinct from the work of the prophet who speaks as the direct mouth piece of God.

4. Exhortation
   a. Literally means to call aside for the purpose of making an appeal.
   b. In a broader sense it means to entreat, comfort, or instruct (Acts 4:36; Heb. 10:25).

5. Giving
   a. The essential meaning is to give out of a spirit of generosity.
   b. In a more technical sense it refers to those with resources aiding those without such resources (2 Cor. 8:2; 9:11–13).
   c. This gift is to be exercised without outward show or pride and with liberality. (2 Cor. 1:12; 8:2; 9:11, 13)

6. Leadership
   a. Refers to the one "standing in front."
   b. Involves the exercise of the Holy Spirit in modeling, super-intending, and developing the body of Christ.
   c. Leadership is to be exercised with diligence.

7. Mercy
   a. To feel sympathy with the misery of another.
   b. To relate to others in empathy, respect, and honesty.
   c. To be effective, this gift is to be exercised with kindness and cheerfulness—not as a matter of duty.

Gifts from God the Son are pivotal in assuring that the gifts from God the Holy Spirit *are activated and functioning in the Church (Ephesians 4:12-13), the Power is in the Flow of the Spirit through the Pattern.*

Gifts of the Son *Ephesians 4:11 (also 1 Cor. 12:28): (To Facilitate and Equip the Body of the Church)*[59]

1. Apostles
   a. In apostolic days referred to a select group chosen to carry out directly the ministry of Christ; included the assigned task given to a few to complete the sacred canon of the Holy Scriptures.
   b. Implies the exercise of a distinct representative role of broader leadership given by Christ.
   c. Functions as a messenger or spokesman of God.
   d. In contemporary times refers to those who have the spirit of apostleship in remarkably extending the work of the church, opening fields to the gospel, and overseeing larger sections of the body of Jesus Christ.

2. Prophet
   a. A spiritually mature spokesman, a proclaimer with a special, divinely focused message to the church or the world, originating from God.
   b. A person uniquely gifted at times with insight into future events.

3. Evangelist
   a. Refers primarily to a special gift of preaching or witnessing in a way that brings unbelievers into the experience of salvation.

---

[59] "Holy Spirit Gifts and Power" by Paul Walker, *Spirit filled life study Bible*. 1997, c1991 (electronic ed.) (Re 22:18). Nashville: Thomas Nelson.

    b. Functionally, the gift of evangelist operates for the establishment of new works or new territories with-in an existing work, while pastors and teachers follow up to organize and sustain.

    c. Essentially, the gift of evangelist operates to establish converts and to gather them spiritually and literally into the body of Christ.

4. Pastor/Teacher

    a. The word pastor comes from a root meaning to protect, from which we get the word shepherd.

    b. Implies the function of a shepherd/leader to nurture, teach, and care for the spiritual needs of the body.

    c. Although combined here the Pastor and Teacher gifts can function independently as a distinct gift.

5. Missionary (some see apostle or evangelist in this light)

    a. Implies the unfolding of a plan for making the gospel known to all the world (Rom. 1:16).

    b. Illustrates an attitude of humility necessary for receiving a call to remote areas and unknown situations (Is. 6:1–13).

    c. c. Connotes an inner (burden) compulsion to lead the whole world to an understanding of Jesus Christ (2 Cor. 5:14–20).

Gifts from God the Holy Spirit are given with a specific purpose to "profit" the Body of Christ. In Greek, to profit is sumphero and means to (bring to fullness, benefit, and give an advantage).

Gifts of the Holy Spirit, *1 Corinthians 12:8–10, 28: (Advancement, Breakthrough and Victory in the Church*[60]

1. Word of Wisdom
   a. Supernatural perspective to ascertain the divine means for accomplishing God's will in given situations.
   b. Divinely given power to appropriate spiritual intuition in problem solving.
   c. Sense of divine direction.
   d. Being led by the Holy Spirit to act appropriately in a given set of circumstances.
   e. Knowledge rightly applied: wisdom works interactively with knowledge and discernment.

2. Word of Knowledge
   a. Supernatural revelation of the divine will and plan.
   b. Supernatural insight or understanding of circumstances or a body of facts by revelation: that is, without assistance of any human resource but solely by dome aid.
   c. Implies a deeper and more advanced understanding of the communicated acts of God.
   d. Involves moral wisdom for right living and relationships.
   e. Requires objective understanding concerning divine things in human duties.
   f. May also refer to knowledge of God or of the things that belong to God, as related in the gospel.

---

[60] "Holy Spirit Gifts and Power" by Paul Walker, *Spirit filled life study Bible*. 1997, c1991 (electronic ed.) (Re 22:18). Nashville: Thomas Nelson.

3. Faith
   a. Supernatural ability to believe God without doubt.
   b. Supernatural ability to combat unbelief.
   c. Supernatural ability to meet adverse circumstances with trust in God's messages and words.
   d. Inner conviction impelled by an urgent and higher calling.

4. Gifts of Healings
   a. Refers to supernatural healing without human aid.
   b. May include divinely assisted application of human instrumentation and medical means of treatment.
   c. Does not discount the use of God's creative gifts (Doctors and Medicine)

5. Working of Miracles
   a. Supernatural power to intervene and counteract earthly and evil forces.
   b. Literally means a display of power giving the ability to go beyond the natural.
   c. Operates closely with the gifts of faith and healings to bring authority over sin, Satan, sickness and the binding forces of this age.

Holy Spirit Gifts and Power by Paul Walker, with Special Emphasis by Prophet Harvey Johnson *Spirit filled life study Bible*. 1997, c1991 (electronic ed.) (Re 22:18). Nashville: Thomas Nelson *Gifts from God the Holy Spirit are given with a specific purpose to "Profit" the Body of Christ. In the Greek to "Profit" is "Sumphero" and means to (Bring to Fullness, Benefit, and Give an Advantage).*

Gifts of the Holy Spirit, *(Continued), 1 Corinthians 12:8–10, 28, (For Advancement, Breakthrough and Victory in the Church)*[61]

6. Prophecy
    a. Divinely inspired and anointed utterance.
    b. Supernatural proclamation in a known language.
    c. Manifestation of the Spirit of God—not of intellect (1 Cor. 12:7).
    d. May be possessed and operated by all who have the infilling of the Holy Spirit (1 Cor. 14:31).
    e. Intellect, faith, and will are operative in this gift, but its exercise is not intellectually based. It is calling forth words from the Spirit of God

7. 7. Discerning of Spirits
    a. Supernatural power to detect the realm of the spirits and their activities
    b. Implies the power of spiritual insight—supernatural revelation of plans and purposes of the Enemy and his forces.

8. Different Kinds of Tongues
    a. Supernatural utterance in languages not known to the speaker: *these languages may be existent in the world*, revived from some past culture, or "unknown" in the sense that they are a means of communication inspired by the Holy Spirit

---

[61] "Holy Spirit Gifts and Power" by Paul Walker, *Spirit filled life study Bible*. 1997, c1991 (electronic ed.) (Re 22:18). Nashville: Thomas Nelson.

(Is. 28:11; Mark 16:17; Acts 2:4; 10:44–48; 19:1–7; 1 Cor. 12:10, 28–31; 13:1–3; 14:2, 4–22, 26–32).

    b. b. Serve as an evidence and sign of the indwelling and working of the Holy Spirit.

9. Interpretation of Tongues
    a. Supernatural power to reveal the meaning of tongues.
    b. Functions not as an operation of the mind of man but as the mind of the Spirit.
    c. Does not serve as a translation (interpreter never understands the tongue he is interpreting), but rather is a declaration of meaning.
    d. Is exercised as a miraculous and supernatural phenomenon as are the gift of speaking in tongues and the gift of prophecy.

Notes[62]: Because all three categories of gifts—the Father's, the Son's and the Holy Spirit's, *involve some expression of "prophecy," it is helpful to differentiate. In this category* (Rom.12) the focus is *general,* characterized by that level of the prophetic gift which would belong to *every* believer—"all flesh." The Holy Spirit's "gift of prophecy" (1 Cor. 12) refers to supernatural prompting, *so much so that tongues with interpretation is equated with its operation* (1 Cor.14:5). The office–gift of the prophet, which Christ gives to His church through individual ministries, is yet another expression of prophecy: those holding this office must meet *both* the Old Testament requirements of a prophet's accuracy in his message, and the New Testament standards of life and character required of spiritual leadership.

The New Testament seems to recognize three
basic types of Administration;

1. The Servant Leader or Deacon: Greek *Diakonia* means service or ministry (Acts 6:1–6; 2 Cor. 9:12).

2. The Leader or Manger: Greek *Oikonomos* or *Oikonomis* means Steward such as today's pastor. The word literally means household manager and refers to those who manage the church. (1 Cor. 4:1, 2; 2 Tim.1:7).

3. The Steersman Leader or Overseer: is found in the office of Apostle or Bishop. *Kybernesis* is a Greek term borrowed from seafaring used to designate the steersman or pilot who holds a ship on course. This word is rendered governments (I Cor.12:28) where Paul speaks of the spiritual gift of administration.

---

[62] "Holy Spirit Gifts and Power" by Paul Walker, *Spirit filled life study Bible*. 1997, c1991 (electronic ed.) (Re 22:18). Nashville: Thomas Nelson.

About the Author

Harvey's spiritual roots are birthed out of the ministry of Apostle Joseph Hobbs, Th. D., Sr. Pastor, and Elder Brenda Hobbs, Co. Pastor at Triumphant Life Christian Church in Highland Park, Michigan.

Having been led by the Spirit, Harvey and his wife Charlotte relocated to Georgia in June 2004, where they also established Remnant Life World Ministries, that was assigned as Church Builders by the Spirit to create and build sustainable foundations for ministries in that area. Harvey and Charlotte continue to carry out their vision in that region.

Operating in the Office and Gifts of the Prophetic, Harvey delivers an irrepressible spiritual clarity in His preaching and teaching of the Word of God and has blessed many lives and ministries across the United States including Detroit, Kansas, New York, Nashville, Virginia, North Carolina, Florida, Augusta, Atlanta, and Alabama.

Harvey previously served on the Executive Board of Bashan Ministries in Queensland, Australia, and continues to be a voice of counsel to many ministries and aspiring spiritual and business leaders.

Harvey holds a BA in Business and a MA in Economics and International Finance. His entrepreneurial acumen is well-known in business circles throughout the United States, South America, Mexico and Europe.